"This book changed my game! I thought I understood tennis, but I didn't. I know the rules, but I didn't know what it takes to win at my level. I appreciate that it's written for the club player – Me! I'll never be great but I want to win and now I am winning more than ever. Most self-improvement books bore me. This one gave me tools I could use and entertained me too. I highly recommend it."

Jill Delp
Colleyville, TX

"Can't thank you enough for your book. Since I read it, I have been beating players much better than me. My secret is reading a part of it before going out to play. Your stories about Bobby Riggs and others are great too. Thanks!"

Gary Rosenblatt
New York, NY

"I thoroughly enjoyed Tennis Tips. Doug's philosophies are right on the mark for all club players, and I believe it can make many a reader a more 'airtight' and tenacious competitor. Plus, it is fun to read about some fascinating adventures."

Doug Lewis
Head Tennis Pro – Quogue Field Club, NY

"Tennis Tips and Tall Tales was highly enjoyable reading. I try to reinforce these basic concepts in my everyday game and guess what? It WORKS! Thanks, Doug, for reminding me how stupid a player too many of us are."

Mike Kaufman
Great Neck, NY

"Tennis Tips and Tall Tales was not only an enjoyable read off the court, but an unbeatable tool on the court. I can't tell you how much help I received from it. I highly recommend this book."

Alyse Margolis
Woodbury, NY

Tennis Tips and Tall Tales

by Doug Dean

Magic Valley Publishers

Sale of this book without a front cover may be unauthorized. If this book is without a cover, it may have been reported to the publisher as "unsold or destroyed" and neither the author nor the publisher may have received payment for it.

Published by Magic Valley Publishers
Copyright 2005 © by Doug Dean
All Rights Reserved.

Except for use in any review, the reproduction of this work in whole or in part in any form by any electronic, mechanical or other means, now known or hereafter invented, including xerography, photocopying and recording, or in any information storage or retrieval system, is forbidden without the written permission of the publisher, Magic Valley Publishers, 6390 E Willow St, Long Beach CA 90815 U.S.A.

ISBN 0-9716681-7-5

Cover design by Matt Gonzalez
Cover photo courtesy of El Dorado Park Tennis Center
Manufactured in the United States of America

DEDICATION

I dedicate this book to my fellow teaching pros. I feel your pain and fatigue at the end of a long day of grinding it out in the sun. I also share in your satisfaction when you know you've really helped someone "get it." I identify with how you labor in obscurity and I salute you.

I wish to acknowledge Sharon Glassmayer, whose persistence resulted in me putting my thoughts and experiences down on paper. Special thanks to my sister Debbie for her editing skills. I would be remiss not to mention Lorne Kuhle, who gave me my first job in the United States as the assistant pro at the MGM Grand Hotel in Las Vegas.

Finally, I rarely teach a lesson without trying to pass on some proverb of tennis truth that I received from the legendary Bobby Riggs. When I reflect on all the interesting conversations and fun tennis matches I was allowed to share with him, it brings a smile to my face. I have yet to find a more unique character on the face of the earth.

Tennis Tips and Tall Tales

CONTENTS

INTRODUCTION

PART ONE – GET YOUR MIND RIGHT
- Chapter 1 - Reality Therapy
- Chapter 2 - The Essence of the Game
- Chapter 3 - Errors – Forced or Unforced
- Chapter 4 - The Dinker
- Chapter 5 - The Patron Saint
- Chapter 6 - Margin of Error
- Chapter 7 - Something Has to Give
- Chapter 8 - Your Best Friend

PART TWO – TECHNIQUE
- Chapter 9 - The Set-Up
- Chapter 10 - Movement - The Great Intangible
- Chapter 11 - Stroking the Ball – Less Is More
- Chapter 12 - Carry the Ball
- Chapter 13 - The Backswing – Easy Does It
- Chapter 14 - The Forehand
- Chapter 15 - The Backhand
- Chapter 16 - The Serve
- Chapter 17 - The Overhead Smash
- Chapter 18 - The Return of Serve
- Chapter 19 - The Net Shot
- Chapter 20 - The Approach Shot
- Chapter 21 - The Lob
- Chapter 22 - The Drop Shot

PART THREE – ASK THE PRO
- Chapter 23 - Should you Change a Losing Game?
- Chapter 24 - What About Practice?
- Chapter 25 - What About Practice Matches?

Chapter 26 - Why do Some Players Never Improve?
Chapter 27 - Should You Change an Incorrect Stroke?
Chapter 28 - How About a Goal?
Chapter 29 - What About Lessons, Camps and Clinics?
Chapter 30 - What About Racquets?
Chapter 31 - Show Some Class

PART FOUR- The GREATEST STROKES I'VE EVER FACED

PART FIVE –THE ADVENTURES OF A NO-NAME PRO

INTRODUCTION

So you want to play some tennis? Good choice for a host of reasons. Tennis is the game of a lifetime. It can be played by all age groups and by all members of the family. Unlike many sports, it is truly international, with great players coming from all over the world. It can be played indoors and outdoors: on clay, grass, carpet and cement.

I grew up in the Midwest. In *my* circles, tennis was thought of as a sissy sport. What a misconception that was! It is truly great exercise. Can you say that about golf? Billiards? Horseshoes? Poker? To most of us, jogging is boring. But there is something about going after a tennis ball that will make you chase it until your tongue is dragging. You're so engaged in the battle that you don't even realize you're getting a great workout.

Tennis is an extremely challenging game on many levels. It will test your agility, stamina, speed, technique and strategy. It differs from a lot of recreational activity with one important distinction — in tennis, you *keep score*. There is a winner and there is a loser. While it is fun to play, I maintain that it is more fun to *win*. That's what I want you to do — have more fun by winning more. That's what this book is about.

I will never be accused of being a great player, nor do I consider myself a master authority of the game. I have, however, taught and observed tennis at the club level for 25 years; I have noticed that a vast majority of club players repeatedly make the same kinds of mistakes, both mental and physical. I have tried to address these mistakes.

Let me say that if you are a college player, or a top young junior on your way up, this material is not for you. You have the speed and power to play the game at the highest level. Instead, this book is for the vast majority of club players who love the game and try to sneak in a match or two on the weekends (or whenever they can find time).

First, I have attempted to give you a mental point of view, as well as theory and philosophy. I hope it can help you immediately as well as give you some direction for the future. I have thrown several concepts into the mix. Some of these may be redundant to you, but if just one or two thoughts click, it might help. Secondly, I have added tips on the various strokes, covering both physical technique and strategy. I have tried not to make these too technical, choosing, rather, to emphasize the most common mistakes on each of the shots. Along these lines, I have included a section that touches on the issues of practice, strategy, camps, racquets, and commonly asked questions. Next, I have listed the greatest strokes I have ever faced during my experiences in the tennis world, the sports world, and the world of entertainment. Finally, I have included a few of my more memorable tales. Tennis has gotten me into a lot of crazy adventures over the years, with a cornucopia of interesting people.

Tennis Tips and Tall Tales

To understand where I am coming from, you need to know my influences. I am lucky enough to have had discussions with tennis "greats" such as Jack Kramer, Poncho Gonzales, Grand Slam winner Don Budge, and Poncho Segura. All of these men were No. 1 in the world players in the 1940's, 50's and 60's, and some of the greatest players of all time. (I was privileged enough to have played with both Ponchos. What a thrill!) Do you know what all these great authorities told me? That the smartest player and the toughest competitor they ever played was Bobby Riggs. *That* got my attention. Why did they say that? Because they lost to him at one time or another.

The first time I went to Bobby's condo in San Diego, I literally tripped over his 73 national championship trophies. In 1939, the one and only time Bobby played Wimbledon, he won the singles, doubles, and mixed doubles titles; and he was the only player to do so in a single Wimbledon. Are those credentials enough? It was part of my tennis odyssey to share an apartment with Bobby for three years in Las Vegas. In the early 80's, I was his head teaching pro at the Dunes Hotel where he was the director of tennis. During that time, Bobby gave me a PhD in back-alley, street-smart, trench-warfare, airtight tennis. What an interesting character! He looked like a goofy non-athlete. He walked like a duck, talked with a funny, raspy voice, and would compliment you as he carved you like a Christmas turkey. It was a thing of beauty to observe. He did it so quietly that you never knew what hit you.

Let me go on record to say that much of what I have to share I learned from Bobby. I only hope that this book will give you the same positive results that Bobby's instruction gave me. I got to play a lot of doubles with Bobby during my time with him at the Dunes. Even though he was in his late sixties, undeniably past his prime, I was continually fascinated with his smooth technique, his shot selection, his discipline, and his concentration. We were able to win a lot of matches against many younger, stronger opponents whom we had no business beating. We did it by applying the same strategies and thought processes that I will attempt to convey to you.

I loved being in a close match with Bobby. If it would get down to four all in the third set, he would lean over and implore, "OK, from here on in we play airtight." I knew exactly what he meant. It is my goal that after you read this book, you, too, will know what airtight means, and can apply it with successful results.

Now, the goal is not to make you into a world-class player — because I don't think this is possible. Rather, I want to challenge you to become a good, smart player who is a great competitor! I want you to start playing more airtight. I want you to stop beating yourself. Let's do away with those suicide losses where your opponent gives you a little rope and let's you hang yourself. I want a lot more wins and only "Smith Barney" losses; that is, where you make your opponent win the old fashioned way: he has to *earn* it. Are you ready?

PART ONE

GET YOUR MIND RIGHT

CHAPTER 1

REALITY THERAPY

There are approximately 15.8 million tennis players in the world. Of that figure, there are perhaps two or three thousand world-class players. Remember, only 120 players are allowed to play Wimbledon and the U.S. Open. The world-class level is the zenith of the game. It showcases a wonderful blend of power, control and speed. It demands that every shot be executed to near perfection on a consistent basis for up to three, and even four, hours at a time.

To achieve this level requires three ingredients: (1) an early start; (2) great talent; and (3) several years of total dedication. There are pro baseball players who did not play in high school or college. There are players in the NFL who did not play football in high school or college. There are players in the NBA who did not play basketball in high school or college. There are even successful pro golfers who didn't start golf until their 20's. *But*, there is not now, nor has there ever been in the history of tennis, a single player who has had any success at the world-class level who didn't start at an early age! By this, I mean, at the very oldest, age twelve or thirteen, and usually much younger. This is one of the main differences with tennis and the other sports. There is a reason why an admission price is charged to go see the U.S. Open —

very few people can hit great shots on a consistent basis.

I will give you an example. I recently went to Florida where I played eleven-year-old Danny Riggs, the grandson of Bobby Riggs. Danny is the No. 1 player in Florida in the 12 and under category. He drills all the shots for hours everyday, including one hundred serves daily. He played 30 tournaments in 2004! He is paying the price and will be one of the very few who will have a shot at success at the world-class level. He is earning the right to be a shot maker with huge power. Do you have that kind of base in your tennis background? The average person has no clue how much sacrifice and total dedication it takes to achieve this level of skill.

Let me be more specific. If you could win just one game off of the worst first round loser in the men, or even women's bracket at the U.S. Open, I would have a lot of respect for your game. That's how much admiration I have for the world-class level player. So, what I am trying to say is, if you fall short in any of the three areas that I just mentioned, then I have some bad news for you: you are not a world-class player and you *never* will be. I don't mean to be pessimistic or a jerk, but rather a realist, and history bears me out. Ironically, I believe that the sooner you understand this and accept your limitations, the sooner you can have more success at the club level.

Club tennis is a *different* game! It requires a certain amount of compromise and practicality. It doesn't require great tennis for success because great players don't play at the club level. They are either flying all over the world trying to win prize money and ATP ranking points, or they are playing serious tournament tennis at the high school and college levels. These real players have their own agenda, their own time frame, and it doesn't include the rest of us. They are going for it. They are the shot makers!

I'm not saying the rest of us can't hit great shots, because many of us can. It's just that we can't do it consistently. That is the *main* difference. We have to pick our spots. Fortunately, winning at the club level doesn't demand great shot making.

Success at club tennis requires a different arsenal. It starts with discipline and demands resourcefulness, mental toughness and heart. For you to develop into a great shot maker is highly improbable. In all likelihood, you don't have the time or the youth required to do so. There is, however, *no reason* not to become a very crafty, intelligent player who gets the very most out of what you have because you are a great *competitor*. A competitor knows what his capabilities are and plays within them. What I am asking you to do is to be *pragmatic* and to be willing to compromise.

There, I told you the bad news. Now for some good news. Most everybody you will ever play in your life is in the same predicament as you. Therefore, you should be capable of competing favorably, to some degree or another, with most anyone you play.

All athletic competition, it seems to me, is a metaphor for real combat; you fight to the death, if necessary, for conquest. Now, if you are in the trenches with a grenade and rifle, do you think you can defeat an armored tank? I don't think so. But you have a chance against another soldier in the other trenches if you battle with a lot of heart and don't take stupid risks. I submit to you that if you were caught in that situation, you would be more interested in victory (getting out of there alive) than how good your uniform looked or how shiny your rifle was as you went down in defeat.

What is tennis to you, Mr. Club Player? It is not getting ready to play Wimbledon. That is not going to happen. Tennis to you is beating Andy Annoying at your club, the guy who wears fancy outfits, carries two racquets, and thinks he is doing you a favor by playing with you. He always beats you about 6-3, 6-3. Beating that level of player is an *achievable* goal. That's the person whom I want to help you beat. Beating that guy will give you every bit as much thrill and enjoyment as Pete Sampras had winning the U.S. Open. That is real tennis for you. That kind of winning will give you *kicks*. That's what I hope this book will help you get - more kicks out of great, hard-fought wins. Do you have in mind those opponents who beat you 6-3? OK! Set your sights on them. Let's go after them. They've been having too much fun at your expense.

CHAPTER 2

THE ESSENCE OF THE GAME

Let's go to the mental blocks that are the biggest hindrances to proficiency at the club level. I believe with all my heart that the single biggest reason that more Club Players don't have more success is that they don't grasp the true *essence of the game*. What is it? The *essence of the game* is that *tennis is a game of errors*! Whoever makes the least number of errors wins. If you don't fully understand and apply this, you will make too many errors. If you make too many errors you will lose to people who should never beat you. Unlike ice skating, you aren't awarded victory because you are judged to have the best form.

Statistically, the evidence is overwhelming. You will make more points from your opponents' errors than from your great shots. You do not get to the next round of a tournament because you hit more winners than your opponent. You get there because you win more points and, almost always, this means that you made *fewer errors*. The *essence of the game* is *not* going to suddenly disappear. If you ignore this, you do so at your own peril. The sooner you accept this reality, the sooner you are going to stop self-destructing as much and improve your game. Please hear me on this! If you don't totally embrace and apply the essence of the game, you will be doomed to a career of inconsistency and the occasional horrendous loss that should *never* have happened.

Why do people make too many errors? Is it because they like to lose? I don't think that's it. There are lots of reasons, but is my core belief that most Club Players are trying to play too much like world-class players. You are trying to look and play like the big name players that you see on TV.

Bobby Riggs was such a colorful character that I could write a book that exclusively featured crazy stories about him. For our purposes here, I will tell you one of my favorites. A friend of mine was playing an international 45 and over tournament in Mexico. Bobby was there to play the 65 and over division. My friend asked Bobby if he would watch him play and give him an evaluation. After my friend lost his match, he asked Bobby for his comments. His answer was this: "Dave, you never *were* a (world class) player, you never *will be* a world-class player, so don't try to *play* like a (world-class) player!" My dear reader, this is the single most *practical* advice I can pass on to you. Dave had beaten himself by making too many errors, trying to hit shots that only a world-class player could consistently hit.

Why are you making too many errors? I would wager a guess that, to some degree or another, you are making the same mistake as Dave, trying to hit world-class shots. Why? It's fun to hit great shots! And I'm not saying don't ever try to. I'm saying don't do it to the extent that you lose to opponents you are capable of beating only by playing smarter and with

Tennis Tips and Tall Tales

more discipline. But before I talk more about errors, I think it is imperative that I make an important distinction.

CHAPTER 3

ERRORS – FORCED OR UNFORCED?

It is very important to know the distinction between forced errors and unforced errors. Some examples: (1) Your opponent hits a fairly hard groundstroke that is deep. You have to run to the other side of the court to hit it. You miss it. That's a forced error. (2) Your opponent comes to the net behind your weak, short ball. You see and hear him coming and you miss your passing shot. That's a forced error. (3) Your opponent hits a hard first serve and maybe it has a good angle on it. You miss it. That's a forced error. In short, whenever your opponent puts pressure on you and forces you to attempt a lower percentage shot, that's a *forced* error. Forced errors are *excusable*. Don't feel that bad about them. You didn't miss an easy shot.

While you always want to reduce forced errors, the name of the game at the club level is to reduce *unforced* errors. What's an unforced error? (1) Double faulting is an unforced error. (2) Your opponent hits a groundstroke that is neither that hard nor that deep, and you miss that shot. You have plenty of time to get set and balanced, and you miss that shot. That's an unforced error. (3) Your opponent hits a fairly weak

Tennis Tips and Tall Tales

second serve and you miss the shot. That's unforced. An unforced error is any shot that you miss when your opponent has not put any pressure on you or put you in a lower percentage shot situation.

Unforced errors are the *scourge* of tennis for the Club Player. To continue to make them is to announce over a loud speaker, *"I don't have a clue how to play!"* I'm shouting now! The single *most important* thing you can ever do to improve your game is to *reduce your unforced errors*! That is the name of the game at the club level. If you are not reducing your unforced errors, I seriously question how much you are improving, even if you are hitting the ball harder all the time.

I have already mentioned the first reason why we make too many errors, but I suspect there is another fundamental reason — making errors just doesn't bother you enough. It is *imperative* that you develop a healthy *disdain* for the unforced error. Until you truly hate making them, you are going to make too many. I have no sympathy for the loss you just sustained because you thought you were having "such a bad day."

If I said to you, "If you miss this next shot, I'm going to rip your next paycheck," would you concentrate a little harder, move your body a little quicker, (to get into better position), swing less hard, and be more careful? *I think so.* If I said to you, "If you don't hit in two balls in a row, I'm going to smash the windshield of your new car with a sledgehammer," do you think you would watch the ball a little better, move a little better, swing a little slower, hit the ball a little better, hit it a little safer, and concentrate a little harder? *I think so.* If I said to you, "If you don't hit in three balls in a row, all of your employees get to go home at noon for a week," do you think you would try a low percentage, screaming winner? *I don't think so.* If in real life you were penalized like this for making stupid errors, would it change the way you play? So fast it would make your head spin.

You have to start hating the unforced error. I have often fantasized about the perfect teaching court. It would be one that would give you a little shock for every time you tried a wild shot. OK, maybe that's a little extreme, but I think it would weed out wild swinging really fast.

CHAPTER 4

THE DINKER

Now, I can hear some of your moaning, "All you are telling me is to become a Dinker." No I am not. I want you to become a well-rounded player who is constantly improving your offensive as well as your defensive skills. But while we are on the subject, let me give you my two cents on the topic. For twenty-five years I have been fascinated to hear people complaining about hating to play the Dinker. They say, "I just can't play against a guy like that....that's not real tennis"....."Play like a man." Have you ever heard that said? I hear it every week.

What is a Dinker? In my mind, the Dinker is a limited, mediocre player who hits with neither pace nor depth, and never tries to end the point. Is that good tennis? No. If you have any proficiency, should you lose to a player like that? No! But here is the misconception. If you lose to a "real player", who "plays like a man" and hits with big power, you don't mind that loss so much because that player was "too good." *But*, if you lose to someone who hits with no pace or depth, it is a sad wake-up call that you can't play as well as you though. Nobody likes that message. Make no mistake about it. If you lose to a Dinker, you lose to someone who may not have as good a game as you, but who is a better *competitor*.

Doug Dean 18

I have a lot of respect and sympathy for the so-called "Dinkers." They at least understand the *essence of the game* and are not going to try something that they can't do. Accordingly, they aren't going to beat themselves. You have to take a match from them with superior skill and equal heart. If you can't beat a Dinker, you aren't doing him a favor by playing. He is doing you one. By far, I would rather be in a foxhole with a good Dinker than a flashy Fence Beater any day of the week, because I know I have a better chance of getting out of there alive.

Rather than dodging the Dinker, you should occasionally go out of your way to seek him out. That's where you get the *true* barometer of your skill level and your ability to compete. If you lose to a Dinker, don't scream and throw your racquet. You should congratulate him and take your beating like an adult. That person just gave you a free lesson about some glaring weaknesses in your game. Hopefully, it will be an incentive to improve your skill level so that you don't have to lose to someone who is not a complete player. Remember, being a great competitor is a key ingredient to success, especially at the club level. Let me give you a couple of examples of great competitors at both levels.

CHAPTER 5

THE PATRON SAINT

Remember Mats Wilander? He emerged from that good crop of Swedish players who came along in the 80's after Borg. Mats didn't have a big serve or a very powerful groundstroke, or even a particularly good net game. But he was very quick, very resourceful, and had the heart of an elephant. In 1988, Wilander beat Ivan Lendl in the finals of the U.S. Open. He beat the No. 1 player in the world, one who had a better serve, a more powerful groundstroke, and had just as good a net game. How is that possible? Mats did it by grinding it out. He hardly ever hit the ball really hard and almost every ball went five or six feet over the net. The match lasted over five very punishing hours, and Wilander won 8-6 in the fifth set.

Do you think that Mats loved exhausting his body like that? Did he hit medium serves because he didn't like big serves? I don't think so. He would have loved to hit big aces but didn't have the talent for it, so he didn't try. Did he love hitting medium balls instead of really hard groundstrokes? I doubt it. He didn't hit really hard groundstrokes because when he did, too often, they went out. What he *could* do, however, was hit twenty medium balls in a row if he had to. Mats realized *that* was what kept him in the match.

Therefore, he was *willing* to do it. His biggest weapons were his mind and his heart.

I will forever be in awe of what Wilander did on that day, because he proved that a very good pro who is a great competitor could beat the No. 1 player in the world on one of the game's biggest stages. Mats Wilander should be the Patron Saint of the Club Players of the world. He played an advance version of club tennis and won the U.S. Open. Now, I submit to you that if that kind of mental toughness and discipline works at the highest level of the game, it will work *more* at the club level. Are you willing to do what you have to do in order to win the match? This is one of the keys to success in airtight tennis. This is how you win in the trenches.

Allow me to give another example that is closer to home for all of us. I submit to you my former pupil, Steve Fox. Steve plays club tennis at various clubs in the Hamptons in Long Island. Steve is a very good athlete who didn't pick up tennis until his thirties, far too late to become a world-class player. He does not have a good serve. He has no net game to speak of, and his forehand is extremely average. He has a very functional slice backhand, a good lob, very good mobility and excellent mental toughness. Steve used to be a member of the Hampton Athletic Club which houses a lot of very good Club Players, some of whom were good former college players. I saw him enter the club tournament which, by all rights, he should have lost in the first round. Instead, he won five straight matches and won the tournament. Here's the kicker — Steve was in his fifties! He was spotting players

Tennis Tips and Tall Tales

sometimes twenty years younger, all of whom had better groundstrokes and better serves. How is that possible? He was so mentally tough that he didn't try one, stupid shot. He made few errors and broke his opponents down. He was willing to do what he had to do in order to win.

Congratulations to Steve Fox. You are a club champion. You didn't have the best game but you were the best player. It is the Steve Foxes of the club world that I most admire and respect, because they are getting the most out of what they are capable of doing and experiencing, the irreplaceable thrill and fun of winning. They have discovered the quiet power of airtight tennis.

Have you locked into the concept of reducing your unforced errors? A very important mental ingredient in doing so is to be much more *careful* about the types of shots you are making. When I taught in Vegas, I noticed that developers kept building new casinos all the time. Apparently, the casino business understands the value of having the odds in their favor. From now on, I want you to begin to approach your tennis game as if you were a blackjack dealer instead of a player. Let's get the odds more in your favor. You need to reduce the number of low percentage shots and increase the number of high percentage shots that you are taking. This is critical to reducing errors. In order to do this, there is a concept you really need to embrace in the next chapter.

CHAPTER 6

MARGIN OF ERROR

To understand *margin of error* and to respect it is to have real insight into the high percentage shot. To not understand it is to play a low percentage game without realizing it. The average club player simply does not allow for enough *margin of error* on his shots. What is it? It is the built-in *safety factor* in your shot.

When you make an error only three things can happen: The ball goes into the net, the ball goes wide, or the ball goes long. Of these three, *by far*, the biggest mistake the club player makes, (and by far the dumbest of the three), is hitting into the net. It breaks my heart to see a club player hit a beautifully stroked ball into the top of the net. The stroke had very little that was wrong with it! It wasn't hit too hard, and it had nice rhythm and tempo. Another inch and it would have been a very good shot. What went wrong? The shot that was attempted was *too low percentage* and required perfect timing. The slightest miscalculation made it go into the top of the net. The mistake was not building enough of a safety factor into the shot, not enough *margin of error*. That same stroke hit three feet higher would have allowed for a lot more miscalculation and would have still gone in. And you know what? It would have been almost as good of a shot as the one that was hit closer to the net.

Tennis Tips and Tall Tales 23

Don't take *unnecessary* risks. It's insane! How many times did I hear Bobby Riggs preach, "Play the safe shot, *safely!*" But all day long, I see the club player play the safe shot unsafely. What is a safe shot? It's one in which you're not trying to hit a winner. You're not even trying to hit an aggressive shot. You're just trying to get it in defensively, but you hit *that* ball into the net! That's crazy! If you're going to play the safe shot, play it *safely*! Allow for *margin of error*. Hit it four, five, or even six feet over the net if you have to, so that there is *no* chance of it going into the net. Don't flirt with disaster. How many times did your mother tell you not to play with fire? Don't get burned by unnecessary risk. If your opponent is in the back court, there is nothing particularly special about your hitting a low, risky ball.

The hardcore reality is that, in a great majority of your shots, the *little* extra pressure that you're putting on your opponent with a lower percentage shot does not merit the *much greater* risk you are taking. Most of the time you're not being rewarded enough for the risk. Would you drive 100 m.p.h. around a winding road to save five minutes of time? Would you do a swan dive from one hundred feet into a shallow pool for ten dollars? No? Not enough reward? So don't take stupid risks in your shots for a marginal reward.

If you're going to take a risk, then make sure that it is really going to count when you execute the shot. Let's say your opponent has come to the net. You don't want him there, but he's there anyway. He's forcing you into taking more risk. *Now* is the time to hit harder and lower. If you execute that difficult passing shot, your risk is going to be rewarded with the point. You should only take a lot of risk in a shot if, by executing it, you will be rewarded by a point, or, at the very least, by being placed into a meaningful advantage in the point. If that isn't the case with your shot, then you shouldn't be trying anything too fancy.

Let's go over some more pragmatic, higher percentage thoughts. Begin to play as if the net were three feet higher than it actually is. In addition to this, pretend that the sidelines are three feet narrower on each side. These mental adjustments allow for a greater *margin of error*. You need to be able to "miss" the down-the-lines shot by three feet and still keep the ball in. I want more and more of your "misses" to go in because you have allowed for more *margin of error*. The ball that goes over the net by six inches should be in because you were aiming three feet over the net and "missed" the shot by two-and-a-half feet, and *not* because it was aimed. It is really important to *understand this distinction*, because you are really playing *smart* when your *misses go in*.

The best way to miss a shot is to miss it long. A long ball is still an error that loses the point. I understand that there is nothing special about this. But a ball that goes into the net has *no chance*. If it goes over the net, it still has a chance. A strong wind might instantly come up and blow it inside the line, or your net-playing opponent might take a swing at a ball that was going out. What I'm getting at here is that by taking fewer low percentage risks that don't pay off, you will begin to reduce greatly the kinds of errors that cause you to miss two-thirds of the time.

Tennis Tips and Tall Tales

Next, most of your groundstrokes should be hit crosscourt. The crosscourt ball is higher percentage because it goes over the lower part of the net into the fatter part of the court. It also makes your opponent run more. You should hit crosscourt 75% of the time. The down-the-line ball goes over the higher part of the net into a smaller part of the court. It should be used when the situation demands it, but it should not carry equal weight. This shot should be used more only if it is exploiting the weak side of your opponent.

Let me repeat this for emphasis: If you miss the shot, miss it long or rarely wide, and never in the net. As a smart, airtight player, your goal is to have a majority of your "misses" go in. From now on, allow for *margin of error*. Respect it. Apply it. It has a lot to do with your mind and your ability to concentrate on the higher percentage shot. Be disciplined about it. Play the percentages like you are the blackjack dealer. Let the odds be in *your* favor. It will *perform* for you. You may not be playing great tennis, but you will be playing good, "smart" tennis; and you will be cutting way down on beating yourself.

CHAPTER 7

SOMETHING HAS TO GIVE

Let's talk a little bit about pace. World class tennis is a wonderful blend of power and control. Isn't it great to blast a big groundstroke for a winner? I love it! It's really fun to do. I just can't seem to do it very often. I have played tennis for thirty years, and I still can't swing very hard and keep it in. I'm no "great player", but I would like to think I'm not the worst athlete in the world. Hitting big offensive shots is just a very difficult thing to pull off consistently. If I could do it more often, I would. The reason I don't try it more is that I like to win. If *you* can hit a lot of big winners, then go for it, but years of observation have taught me to strongly suspect that you probably can't do it either. As a matter of fact, I'm hoping that if we play, you are going to try a lot of big winners (or offensive shots).

The big dilemma for the club player is that you don't have the skill or the timing to hit it as hard as you would like to, and keep it in consistently. So the *compromise* is to tone down the low percentage power shots and to carefully pick the spots when you play offense. For the Club Player, good tennis, predominately, should mean *less* power and more control. I am amazed when I see some teaching pros imploring their pupils to be more aggressive. The poor pupil can't hit in three balls in a row and the pro is

Tennis Tips and Tall Tales   27

telling him to hit it harder! I understand what the pro is going for. I'm not unaware that being aggressive is ideal; but not if you don't have the timing to hit the shots. I guess I just have a higher percentage take on it. If something has to give (and it does), I think you should *always* sacrifice power and never sacrifice control. Most club players constantly violate this precept to the tune of too many errors.

At the world class level, big offense rules — screaming winners and 130 m.p.h. serves. At the club level, however, it's been my observation that quality *defense* is more effective. That's no fun, you say? If you like to blast away, go ahead. Knock yourself out. Take out your frustrations. You don't play tennis for a living, so do whatever is fun. Just don't complain when you have bad losses and don't gripe when players don't want to play with you. Tennis is not like home run derby. You are penalized instead of being rewarded for hitting it out of the park.

So, how hard should you hit the shot? Only you can determine that. It depends on where you are with your skill level and timing. You need to be smart about it and *realistic* about your self-appraisal. Again, Bobby Riggs had the best answer to that question that I ever heard: "Hit the ball as hard as you can while knowing that it's going to go in *every time*." Does that mean to never go for an offensive shot? No. Bill Tilden was the No. 1 player in the world for twenty years during the 20's and 30's. He said, "The only time to try an offensive shot is when you can give yourself a *reasonable* chance of success." I can tell you this — if you are off balance and on the back foot, it is no time to play offense. You are not giving yourself a "reasonable chance."

My rule of thumb: The more difficult the shot and the more you have to run, the less pace you should hit it with and the higher over the net it should go. The easier the shot and the more time you have to prepare, the harder you can hit it, and maybe a little lower. If I haven't played for a month, I hit it higher and slower, because my timing is so bad that I'm required to do this to keep the ball in play. I'm not too proud to do it. If I'm playing everyday for two weeks, I'm hitting the ball significantly harder and a little lower, because my timing is much better. But *never* during that time will I increase my unforced errors. You earn the right to lower your *margin of error* by regular play and increased timing.

There are a lot of levels in tennis. (Today, they call these 3.5, 4.5, etc,). You are playing smart when you are playing within your own capabilities, and when you know what your own level is — as opposed to trying to play one or two levels above where you are. Don't get sucked into trying to play at a higher level if you are not ready to. Don't let your opponent intimidate you into trying to do what you can't do consistently. You are better off making your opponent earn his points. Get real *stingy*...Give away *nothing*!

It was a great discovery for me to learn that you don't have to hit the ball that hard to beat most people, if you can keep the ball in play. Here is what happens. Your opponent subconsciously is counting on you making a lot of unforced errors. When he has to

Tennis Tips and Tall Tales   29

continually hit good shots to win points, it significantly increases the amount of pressure on him. I am constantly amazed at how many players will roll over and collapse with just a little more pressure. That's your job. Apply a little more pressure. You can do it *immediately* if you put your mind to it.

Once, I was doing a clinic with Bobby Riggs in the Hamptons and we were advocating this airtight approach. A Club Player came up to me and said, "I don't really believe you, but I'm going to try that style in my match this afternoon." The next day he came up to me with a big smile on his face. Sure enough, he had beaten a guy he had never beaten before by emphasizing control over power. Did he play great? Probably not — but he got down in the trenches, played airtight, and had some fun winning.

One time while teaching at the MGM Grand in Las Vegas, I was teaching a lesson to a typical Fence Beater. He was swinging way too hard for his level and every other ball was going out. I tried to point out to him that you don't have to hit the ball that hard to beat most people, but he was not buying it. I said to him, "What if I hit the serve to you underhand, I'm not allowed to win the point unless I hit every ball right back to you, and then win 6-0? Would you believe me then?" He said, "Yes, but you can't do that." I replied, "But what if I could — would you believe it?" "Yes, but you can't", he reiterated. Well, as you can guess, I beat him 6-0 and earned his respect. (I even got a fifty-dollar tip.) More importantly, he learned something about keeping the ball in play.

Doug Dean

Erratic power is *overrated*. Don't be overly impressed with it. To the untrained eye, it looks a lot more imposing than it actually is. The medium ball that keeps coming back is the "Rodney Dangerfield" of tennis. It gets no respect. All it does is win. Let's get more specific about steadiness.

CHAPTER 8

YOUR BEST FRIEND

In order to be constantly improving and having success, it's not enough to just keep the ball in play. This is where I draw the distinction between the Dinker and the quality Club Player. The Dinker keeps the ball in play with no pace and no depth. The good Club Player hits a medium ball with reasonably good *depth*. The extra depth makes *all* the difference! The deep ball is the Club Player's "*best friend*." Show me a Club Player who can hit five medium deep balls in a row and I will expect to find a few trophies in that person's house. The deep ball isn't flashy and it usually doesn't finish a point, but it is a deceptively powerful tool. When it can be produced consistently, it is a lethal assassin. It makes your unsuspecting opponent think he's having a bad, unlucky day.

Listen to me! Very few Club Players can stand up to the constant barrage of medium deep balls, no matter how little pace. How do I know? Because I'm not that good, and yet I've beaten hundreds of Club Players by doing this. You don't believe me? Then please, look me up and let's play for dinner. (We're talking steak and lobster here, not Big Macs. It needs to hurt a little)

What is a deep ball? The service line should be your barometer. Don't be happy with any ball that doesn't go *past* the service line. A short ball is always better than an error, but it is not a good shot. A medium ball that goes three or four feet past the service line is a very *respectable* shot. If you can hit it several times in a row, you are really *on* to something. Guess what? To be able to consistently hit medium deep balls is a *realistic*, achievable goal of every Club Player. It is, however, not nearly as easy as it looks. It requires good footwork, good technique, and good concentration. But it *is* achievable. What I want you to develop is a *mind* set that you are *not satisfied* as a player until you can achieve this. Believe me, you haven't "arrived" until you do. I'm dying for you to experience the power of it! Trust me — nine out of ten decent Club Players will roll over and die for you if you can master medium deep balls.

Why is the medium deep ball so powerful? Sooner or later, it causes your opponent to hit the ball off balance, (because of less time to get into position), which creates errors or short balls. The short ball from your opponent gives you much more time to get into position to hit another deep ball. OK, I hear what you are asking, "What if the ball keeps coming back to you with reasonable depth?' Now you have a real challenge because you're playing a good, smart player and you may be forced to try more. The point is this: there is no need to try to play lower percentage offense unless you are absolutely forced to. If you can out-steady someone, there is no need to reinvent the wheel. Most of the time, when playing a good player, you've got to dig a deeper foothold in the trenches and

Tennis Tips and Tall Tales

prepare to work really hard. If not, you're probably going to go down.

Don't get me wrong. There is a lot more to tennis than just hitting medium deep balls. But I honestly believe it is the single *most* important skill you can develop for success at the club level. Become *depth* oriented. Consistent groundstrokes hit past the service line from both sides should be the *foundation* that all other shots and strategies revolve around. Until this foundation is secure, your game is way too vulnerable. What are the necessary skills required to consistently produce medium deep balls? There are three ingredients: balance, footwork and technique. OK! Do I have your mind right? Let's get more specific about how to do it....

Doug Dean

PART TWO

TECHNIQUE

Doug Dean

CHAPTER 9

THE SET-UP

There is an ideal set-up to hitting a tennis ball. It is to be sideways to the net with your weight transferred onto the front leg with good balance. You need to be hitting the ball at waist level or slightly below, without being crowded or rushed. This is the ideal set-up for hitting a groundstroke *every time*. If you can create this set-up, you have greatly reduced the difficulty of the shot that you are about to hit. It is harder to miss an easy shot than it is a hard shot. The goal of your footwork, then, is to create the ideal set-up *every time* you hit the ball. It can't really be done, but the extent to which it can be achieved properly will have a lot of impact about how successful you are in your match.

Of course, the reverse is true for your opponent. You want him to get bad set-ups. By making your opponent run three or four times from side to side, you make it increasingly difficult for him to create the good set-up. The war of attrition is setting in. Sooner or later, your steady play will cause a bad set-up. When you don't have a good set-up, all *hell* breaks loose with your tennis game. By hitting the ball deeper, you increasingly are making your opponent hit off of the back foot rather than the front foot. Again, this greatly increases his difficulty and causes problems. Doesn't this make sense? Are you with me?

Consistently creating good set-ups is one of the real secrets of tennis. You need to be doing it. This is the truly *athletic* part of the game. The baseball batter can dig in and take his time getting set to hit the pitch. The golfer can stand over the ball until he is comfortable. But we poor tennis players only have split seconds to get ready. I think achieving a good set-up is the hardest part of the game. It takes a great deal of energy and concentration to position your body fast enough to create the good set-up. It takes effort and talent, but mostly it takes heart. This is where you show your *true desire* and competitive fire.

The better you get as a player, the more you understand that the greatest expenditure of energy in a tennis match should be used toward creating good set-ups and not actually toward stroking the ball. Stroking the ball should predominately be done smoothly and effortlessly. The average Club Player, however, does just the opposite of this, not spending nearly enough energy towards getting a good, balanced set-up. The average Club Player spends way too much energy hitting the ball, usually too quickly, too hard, and with too much tension in the swing — resulting in what? All together now! Unforced errors.

If you are crowded and unbalanced, (bad set-up), the shot you just missed was not an easy shot. I don't care if it came to you one mile an hour and ten feet over the net; if you were on the back foot, or crowded, or in between steps when you hit it, it was not

Tennis Tips and Tall Tales

an easy shot. It could have been and it *should* have been one! But by not expending the extra energy needed to get into position, you greatly increased the possibility of error. You become the blackjack player instead of the dealer. The odds are not in your favor.

Look at the other sports. How many times have you seen a baseball player get a hit when he swings at a pitch around his head? Most interceptions are thrown when quarterbacks are on the dead run, and thrown in between steps, or off balance. All good shooters in basketball square up their shoulders and collect their balance. When they don't, they usually miss. When is the last time you saw Tiger Woods hit a three-hundred yard drive off of his back foot? On the "twelfth of never." The need for a good set-up seems to be a fundamental law in all sports, and tennis is certainly no exception.

Isn't one of the main reasons you play the game for good, healthy exercise? Do you want a good workout when you play? Do you *really*? Then spend more energy getting your body into proper position — turned, comfortable, creating the waist-high ball off the front foot. *Create an easier shot.* It is very hard to do consistently. It is all the challenge you will *ever* need in tennis. It takes energy, and when you are fatigued, it takes guts. But it pays tremendous dividends. Getting into proper position is the single most underrated physical thing you can do to reduce errors and hit with greater depth.

Granted, quite often you simply do not have the time to get in great position. That's the whole point of moving your opponent, so that he won't have enough time to set-up properly. However, when you do have the time to set up and, for what ever reason, you don't do it and *then* miss a routine shot? *That* is an inexcusable mistake for which you will get no sympathy from me. It is sloppy and lazy; and I don't want to hear that you're having a bad day. You are creating your bad day by not making the effort to get in good position. Obviously, the key ingredient to getting into good position is movement.

CHAPTER 10

MOVEMENT — THE GREAT INTANGIBLE

How important is movement? Once your strokes are established, (and with most players, they never fully are), then movement is the *next most* important part of the game. If you show me two players who have the exact same strokes, and one of them is a half-step quicker, it is likely that the quicker person can win 50 straight times. This is how critical I think that half step is. Do you ever wonder what ever happened to a guy like Ivan Lendl? He was No. 1 or 2 in the world for eight years and then, almost overnight, he could hardly win a first round match and had to retire. What happened? Did he lose those incredible strokes? I don't think so. Did he forget how to compete under pressure? No, he lost a half-step, and it caused everything to break down.

The most amazing thing to me about Jimmy Connors was not his great two-hand backhand, but his ability to cover the court, even into his forties. His mobility was incredible. The main difference in the top twenty players in the world and those ranked around 300, is not stroke production, but movement. The current No. 3 in the world, Layton Hewitt from Australia, doesn't have the best strokes but he is the fastest guy in the game. The Williams sisters have power, but the underrated part of their success is their exceptional court coverage.

Understand something. Tennis is about *running*. The Club Players that I see having the most success are the ones with decent strokes and very good court coverage. If you don't like to run, you are playing the *wrong game*. End of story. Take up golf. Throw darts. Shoot skeet. Go fishing.

If you don't mind running but, for whatever reason, (such as you can't do it very well), you are fighting an up-hill battle. I'm not saying you can't win the game, but tennis is a much harder game for you. You may be forced to play a lower percentage power game because you can't cover the court in long rallies. Conversely, if you can show me a student who has quickness and agility, I will show you a student with a huge, upside potential.

Let's talk about the biggest mistakes. By far, the biggest footwork error that I see the Club Player consistently making is *over striding*. In other words, don't cover the court with steps that are way too big. Inevitably, this results in you getting to the ball in between strides or overrunning the ball, ultimately placing you way too close to it when you have to hit it. This makes you hit the ball off of the back foot, which almost always causes you to hit the ball short. Being off balance translates into having a *lack of depth*. The more correct way to move is with smaller shuffle steps, not unlike a basketball player playing defense. Little shuffle steps should allow you to save room for a final bigger step onto the front leg, giving you balance, weight transfer and body control.

The second big mistake is not getting back to the middle of the court fast enough. The split second you finish a controlled follow-through, you should quickly shuffle back to the middle of the court. Don't stand there flat-footed, admiring your shot, because you don't have time for it. By getting back quickly, you greatly increase your chances of achieving a good set-up for the next ball. Good footwork takes effort. Move your butt! Take the piano off your back! I want to hear rubber burning!

Even if you don't move that well, you can greatly improve your court coverage by anticipation. Good anticipation comes with experience, but mainly with concentration. It is the mental part of court coverage. Paying attention to your opponent's tendencies can get you a big jump on where his next ball is going, thus making you quicker to the shot.

In 1939, when Bobby Riggs was in his prime as No. 1 in the world, he could run a one-hundred yard dash in ten seconds flat. That speed was huge factor in his success. When I played a lot with Bobby, he was in his late sixties and the speed was gone, but his anticipation was uncanny. It allowed him to cover the court much better than the average player with the same speed. Chris Evert was not particularly quick but she had outstanding anticipation. If you develop it, it will buy you some time and help you create some more good set-ups.

How do you improve your ability to move on the court? The sad reality is that if you are very slow, you are never going to be really quick. As the proverb goes, "You cannot put in what God left out." Nature can be cruel, but everybody can improve his or her movement to a certain extent. For the world-class player, special training is no longer optional – it's mandatory. Weight training for strength and stretching exercises for flexibility can, and will, increase quickness and endurance.

In my early forties I took a series of very demanding power yoga classes three times a week for a few months. For me, it turned the clock back and I was moving on the court better than I had in years. I stopped taking the classes because of scheduling conflicts, and immediately my tennis got worse because I couldn't move as well.

By the way, when is the last time you saw someone 15 pounds overweight win a tournament? It never happens. Andre Agassi lost interest for awhile and became out of shape. His ranking dropped below 100. He then embarked on a very strict weight training and exercise program, and climbed back to No. 2 in the world. Lindsey Davenport never won a major tournament until she lost twenty pounds. Martina Navratilova was an immensely talented underachiever until her friend, Nancy Lieberman, placed her on a tremendous conditioning program of weights, stretching and diet. What did she do after that? She won almost every match for five years. Martina remained a fitness fanatic and recently won the 2004 Australian Open mixed doubles title at 46!

Tennis Tips and Tall Tales

In 1973, Bobby Riggs, at the age of 55, played the No. 1 player in the world, Margaret Court, on national television. Bobby had gotten himself into good playing condition and was fortunate to win the match 6-2, 6-1. Two months later, he would play 29-year-old Billie Jean King, the No. 2 woman in the world, in front of the whole world (60 million viewers). Bobby had been playing very little tennis for twenty-five years and, suddenly, during the build-up for the *Battle of the Sexes* match, he was the man of the hour. He was on the cover of *World Tennis, Sports Illustrated* and *Time Magazine*, all at the same time. He was on the TV program, *60 Minutes*, and was in big demand for commercials and for a host of TV talk shows. Bobby was wined and dined, and was flying all over the country making a lot of money for personal appearances. He promoted the *Battle of the Sexes* match beautifully, but he *didn't train enough for it*. Uncharacteristically, he didn't think he needed to. In Bobby's history, he had rarely made the mistake of underestimating his opponent; ironically, however, on this infamous occasion, his gross misjudgment was a classic case of doing just that.

Billie Jean King, on the other hand, left the women's tour and got into the best shape of her life. Bobby went into the match ten pounds heavier than against Margaret Court, and he got trounced. The next time you play, put on a ten-pound weight jacket and see how well you move. Give Billie Jean King credit; she rose to the occasion and all of her hard work paid off. Bobby Riggs won 73 national titles including two U.S. Opens. In his legacy, however, he is known for *one* thing only, losing to a woman in front of the whole world. It cost him several million dollars in endorsements and future match fees. Talk about being penny rich and pound foolish! For the next twenty years, Bobby was haunted by the fact that he played that match unprepared. He would go to his grave thinking that he could have won if he were in the same shape as he was against Margaret Court. Believe me, I know, because I had countless conversations with him about it. The racquet that he used in that match is *hanging on my wall*!

What did that match do for tennis? On the night of the match there were three hundred indoor clubs in the United States. Two years later, there were over 10,000 indoor clubs. It gave me a lot of no-name guys like myself a job. Thank you, Bobby.

In Europe, I got a big-time lesson on the power of movement. I was playing a tournament in Holland against a guy whom I thought I would have no problem beating. Why? He had no serve and a weak backhand. What I didn't realize in the warm-up was that he was the fastest guy I had ever played. He had a great forehand; so obviously, I would hit it to his backhand. He was so fast that he could run around his backhand to hit a forehand, and then get back to the middle. On a hard court, I could have exploited his weaknesses much more easily, but on that slow clay I had a terrible time making him hit a backhand. I lost to a player who only had one stroke and a terrific pair of legs. It was an eye opening display of the power of excellent court coverage.

Tennis Tips and Tall Tales

Anything you *can* do, whether it is lifting weights, jogging, stretching, or dieting... *anything* you can do to improve your ability to cover the court will add immensely to your potential. It is the single best, non-tactical action you can take to improve your game. It is the great intangible.

CHAPTER 11

STROKING THE BALL – LESS IS MORE

Before I get into the specifics of the individual strokes, let's talk about the concept of stroking. My definition of a quality stroke is this: *maximum* results from a *minimum* of effort. The better you get at tennis, the more you should develop the learned skill of *stroking* instead of *hitting*. What is the difference? Hitting implies unnecessary tension, force and muscle. Quality stroking utilizes less muscle and more rhythm, timing and tempo. A good stoker allows the racquet to do more and more of the work. It is a skill that you can consistently improve. Any unskilled player can strike a ball hard if he puts a lot of effort into the hit.

The ultimate purpose of a quality stroke is to allow you to have your cake and eat it too. In other words, a great stroker can hit the ball reasonably hard without swinging too hard. This is higher percentage because it is *repeatable*. And it is achievable. Success at the club level is not hitting great shots but *avoiding* having to hit great shots (way too low percentage). You do that by being able to consistently hit *good* shots; and you do *that* by quality stroking as opposed to hitting.

Tennis Tips and Tall Tales

What is involved in stroking? You cannot be too rich or too thin, or too young; and you cannot hit a tennis ball too smoothly. Smooth is beautiful. It is gorgeous. It is delicious, and, oh yeah, it greatly enhances a consistency. In twenty-five years of teaching I have never admonished a pupil by saying, "Don't swing so smoothly" — never once. But untold thousands of times I have heard myself saying, "Not so quick! Not so tight! Not so much tension!"

Good stroking is *reducing* wasted motion and unnecessary effort. A tight, jerky swing is an unforced error waiting to happen. *Hitting* the ball means you are striking the ball with too much upper body muscle. Stroking the ball means you are emphasizing the muscles in your thighs as you transfer your weight forward. Pace should be generated by weight transfer and hitting the ball out front with good timing, not by using unnecessary force with your arms and shoulders.

Today's racquets are marvels of technology. They are very light and powerful, and don't need a lot of help. Let the racquet do the work. Get the tension out. Transfer all the energy down to the head of the racquet. Relax your arm muscles. Have a firm grip but not a death grip. The best compliment I get from time to time is, "It looks like you aren't trying when you hit the ball." What that person was observing was that my racquet was doing as much of the work as possible. You should constantly be striving to get more out of less. Quality stroking is *fun* to do and *beautiful* to watch. It not only *looks* good, it *feels* good. Your body is telling you that it is right. You can feel the correctness of it. It is a part of the aesthetic joy of playing the game. *Quality execution is its own reward.*

Give yourself credit when you have stroked the ball well. You just hit a good shot. You may have lot the point, but you executed the stroke with quality. Recognize the difference. If you win the point after not stroking the ball well, give yourself credit for competing but don't be happy with the stroke. Only take satisfaction with a quality-executed stroke. By taking this approach, more often than not, you will find that improved depth and consistency are the tangible results. Now, let's talk about one of the secrets to developing the skill of stroking.

CHAPTER 12

CARRY THE BALL

The concept that has helped many of my pupils improve in the art of stroking is the *learned* skill of making the ball *stay* on the strings. If you hit the ball with a tight, jerky stroke, the ball leaves the strings prematurely. It might turn out to be a great shot, but you are always hoping for the best. You can take the guesswork out of it by lengthening the amount of time the ball stays on the strings. The idea is not to hit the ball, but to "catch" it on the strings and "carry" it over to the other side. I believe the longer you can carry the ball, the more you can control where it is going.

How do you do it? Try to absorb the ball and caress it with a stroke that is smooth, clean, fluid and medium. Using a medium tempo is beautiful. It gives you the best chance to hold the ball on the strings. You cannot get too good at it! Make it a goal of your game to become proficient at holding the ball on the strings. This does wonders for your consistency and depth. When I am in proper position to hold the ball on the strings, I feel like I can hit one hundred in a row; and I am surprised when the ball doesn't go in.

What does this skill do to your game emotionally and tactically? I believe that as you develop the ability to carry the ball, it takes away the unnecessary sense of urgency to end the point. When my strokes were immature, I hated long points. They scared me. Do they scare you? As I developed the skill of the "carry", I liked playing longer points more and more. I think you will, too. I want you to get to a place mentally where you don't care that the point is continuing, because you can just carry another deep ball again. I want you to view the long point as something that *favors* you instead of something that punishes you. It's like the surfer on the wave. He knows he's going to fall off but he wants the ride to be as long as possible. You know the point is going to end — you just want to be the one who doesn't fall off first!

What are we talking about here? The length of time that carried ball stays on the strings, as opposed to the harshly struck ball that leaves prematurely, might only be a fraction of a second, but it makes a *huge* difference. I marveled at how well Bobby Riggs carried the ball on his slice backhand. It was so quiet that I could hardly hear the point of contact.

I do not fear the erratic power player. You shouldn't either. Unless he is having a great day, he can be had all day long. No, the players I fear are the ones who hold the ball on the strings. When I see my opponents bring this stroking skill to the table, I know it's time to put my helmet on and dig deep in the trenches, because I'm in for a battle. If I'm not ready to fight hard, then I'm going down.

Remember, medium tempo is beautiful. Don't make your strokes medium rare — just your steaks! Learn how to hold the ball on the strings. Recognize

Tennis Tips and Tall Tales

when you did and did not do it. Get better at it all the time. Take the mystery out of whether the ball is going in or not. If you carried it on the strings, you didn't over hit it, and allowed for enough *margin of error*, it *has* to go in almost every time.

CHAPTER 13

THE BACKSWING – EASY DOES IT

One of the key ingredients to developing a quality stroke is to *avoid being rushed*. You never want to feel like you are in a hurry to make the swing. The best way to accomplish this is to develop the habit of the *early backswing*. It is one of the very best habits you can learn. The second you see from which side the ball is coming, begin taking the racquet back. You can't do this too soon. It should be done with no tension and very little muscle, almost as if you are going to drop the racquet. The early backswing sets the tone for the stroke and gives you a chance at the all-important medium tempo. A late backswing forces a rushed stroke and a rushed stroke is a tension-filled swing.

How should you execute it? You can "loop" it, which is a semi-circular movement, or you can take it straight back, whichever works for you. Personally, I like the loop. Whatever you do, *don't cheat it*! Take it all the way back. Most Club Players don't take enough backswing. If it is too short, it makes you punch and slap the ball too much. Two-thirds of the shot should be completed at the point of contact. When you are running for a shot, begin the backswing while you are on the run. Don't wait until you get to the ball. It's too late then.

CHAPTER 14

THE FOREHAND

This stroke should be your bread and butter shot. It needs to be fundamentally sound and very repeatable. For most people, the forehand should be your best shot. It should allow you to play offense when the situation calls for it. How do you hit it?

In a perfect world, every forehand should be hit *low to high*. Get your racquet head well under the ball, swinging up and through the ball, following through high — even over your shoulder, if that feels good. The low to high swing is the offensive swing. It allows for the greatest possible power and depth. A prerequisite for this swing is the good set-up. An offensive, low to high forehand should be hit "flat" or with "topspin." Two of the greatest players of all time, Jimmy Connors and Chris Evert, both hit flat forehands. If you choose this stroke as your forehand, you need an eastern forehand grip and a locked wrist.

Today's racquets are very light and very strong. They are very conducive to topspin. Therefore, I think that a quality *topspin* forehand should be the goal of every Club Player (unless you have a great feel for the flat stroke). The great topspin forehands of guys like Agassi, Federer and Nadal are hit with an extreme western grip. It works great for these guys because they have hit millions of balls and have earned the right to use it. Now, here is the problem with the western grip: a *very risky* grip for the Club Player because it requires a higher level of timing. It is a high-risk, high-reward grip that produces a lot of great shots, but also a lot of errors.

What I recommend is a "modified" western grip (in between eastern and western). It requires less perfect timing but allows for wrist action, which is conducive to hitting topspin. This grip can allow for a more open stance, but I firmly believe your weight should be moving forward even if your shoulders are not completely turned to the net.

How do you hit topspin? Get the racquet under the ball and brush upward with a *controlled* wrist action. You get into trouble when the wrist action is too quick or too tight. Those are the most common mistakes that I see. The advantage of the topspin is that it allows you to swing a little harder and still keep it in. You need to be disciplined about it. If you don't have a really good set-up, you shouldn't be trying to crack a big topspin winner.

Compactness is good for your stroke. Keep your hand and elbow close to your body. It allows for more control of the swing. If you have to reach for the ball, try to reach with your front leg and not your arm. When you arm is stretched out too far, it causes you to lose wrist control. Also, I see a lot of Club Players with too much of a flat line drive arc to their stroke. That's not good because it's too unforgiving. Low to high is the better way to go. Hit *up* on the ball. Assuming the set-up is there, get well under the ball and *lift* it. You

Tennis Tips and Tall Tales

would do well to copy the stroke of Mats Wilander. He hit the ball four or five feet over the net every time with a medium controlled topspin. He won seven major championships with it.

In a perfect world, you would swing low to high on every forehand. But what if the set-up is not there? What if you are caught with the ball up around your shoulder and it's too late to create the waist level ball? Now it is time to abbreviate the stroke and go *high to low*. Hitting this shot is *admitting* that you are caught out of position and have to switch into defensive survival mode. The high to low shot should be hit with *backspin* and applied with a *locked* wrist. You *have* to have this shot and most Club Players don't use it enough. It can get you out of trouble when you are in a jam. It can keep you alive in the point while you are scrambling to be able to hit it low to high the next time.

The "slice" forehand is used when there is no time to get fancy. Don't try to hit it too hard. Just try to get it deep in order to buy time to get back to the middle of the court. This is a safe shot, so remember to play the safe shot safely! Don't play offensive with a defensive shot. I see this mistake a lot. A good slice forehand is an essential component for your arsenal to do well down in the trenches. Don't be too proud to use it. All I can tell you is, the older I get and the slower I am, the more I use the slice forehand. If you don't have this shot I think you are in big trouble.

CHAPER 15

THE BACKHAND

Physiologically, the backhand is an easier shot to hit than the forehand because it is a natural, unwinding motion. But for a great majority of Club Players, the backhand is weaker than the forehand. Why is that? I believe it is because, for most people, the hand-eye coordination is weaker on the backhand side for the first few months, (maybe years), which causes you to crowd the ball.

If you are a beginner or a struggling intermediate with a very weak backhand, you may strongly want to consider the two-hand backhand, especially if you are a woman with weaker wrists. It is definitely worth experimenting with, but is not for everybody. I start all beginning women and all kids with a two-hand stroke. Why? It is much easier to switch from a two-hander to a one-hander stroke than from a one-hander to a two-hander. The two-hander is mostly hit flat or with topspin. It is a *low to high* swing.

The advantage of the two-hander is that it can develop into a valuable offensive weapon. Using this stroke, you can hit sharper, angle cross-court shots with pace that can really put a lot of pressure on your opponents. The downside to this shot is that it requires more perfect set-ups, and you definitely lose reach.

Tennis Tips and Tall Tales 59

The grip for all backhands is the eastern backhand grip. This is non-negotiable.

If you have a one-hand backhand, then, by far, the most *valuable* shot you will ever possess is the *slice* backhand. I can't tell you how strongly I feel about this. Don't get me wrong; the flat and topspin backhands are more offensive and are great to have, but they require more perfect timing and should only be considered when the set-up is there. The shot that gets you out of trouble when you are out of position is the slice. It is a *lifesaver*. It gives you a chance to get any ball, no matter how hard it is.

The average Club Player tries way too many fancy topspin backhands from difficult situations. That's an error waiting to happen. I'm not saying to never attempt those shots; I'm saying don't try them in the low percentage situations. If you're caught with the ball at your shoulders, slice it *every time*. If you are jammed, and crowded, or the ball got behind you, slice it *every time*. If you are on the dead run or are pulled way wide out of the court, slice it *every time*. Do you ever get caught in those situations? What ? You, too?

With the slice, you always have a chance to keep the ball in play. It enables you to cup the ball and, therefore, hold the ball on the strings longer. It is much safer and requires less perfect timing. It is like the jab to a boxer. You should jab, jab, jab, and then, when there is an opening, go in for the kill, (topspin or flat). But you can't go for the kill all the time. You have to set it up by moving the ball around.

Ken Rosewald was a top ten player in the world for twenty years. He sliced one hundred per cent of his backhands. Steffi Graff won over twenty major titles; she sliced one hundred percent of her backhands. If these players weren't too proud to do it, you shouldn't be either.

I got to spend a day playing with Evonne Goolagong at her club in Hilton Head, South Carolina. She is the only mother ever to have won Wimbledon. She had a great topspin backhand. The year before she won her second Wimbledon, Evonne had taken a long break in order to have her son. She told me that after she had her child, she practiced less and *never* felt she had enough timing to do anything but *slice* the backhand. If a Wimbledon champ was thinking like that, is it possible that you might be trying to make a few too many wild topspin winners?

Now, I want to make a clear distinction between a good quality slice backhand and one that is bad quality. A bad one is a *high to low* chop. It is too quick and too tight. I see a lot of these. The stroke finishes below your knees. With this stroke, you are working too hard and not getting enough results; it produces short balls.

A quality slice is a *high to low to high* stroke. After a good upper body turn and backswing, the racquet starts out slightly above the ball; it comes down and through the ball, but then finishes back upward over your shoulder. A quality slice backhand finishes *up*! That's where the depth comes! Don't chop the ball with tension. That's a hack. Develop a smooth, high to

Tennis Tips and Tall Tales

low to high stroke applied with a *locked wrist*. You can't get too good at this shot. It's money in the bank. It can enable you to stay in a match when you are having a bad day.

If you don't have a good slice backhand in your game, it is certainly not time to increase the amount of offensive shots that require more perfect timing (flat and topspin). What is an adequate slice backhand? As far as I'm concerned, if you can't hit ten balls in a row past the service line, you're not ready to move on.

Recently, Hallmark Entertainment CEO, Robert Halmi, Jr., hired me to help improve his game. He bought into the high percentage, airtight mentality. When we started, he couldn't hit in three backhands in a row. We hit thousands of balls; and then, on one of the last sessions, we had a rally in which he hit 437 slice backhands in a row! Do you think he might be a little tougher to beat today?

Consider a friend of mine in the Hamptons, Barry Wein, who has taken lessons for several summers. He was not blessed with much athletic talent and possessed below average balance. Was tennis hard for you? It was twice as hard for him. When we started, Barry had no backhand whatsoever, but he worked very hard to develop a beautiful slice backhand. He has gone from a guy who no one wanted to play with, to a very in-demand doubles partner, climbing up the ladder. Barry has more and more amazing wins every summer. Think he isn't enjoying his tennis more?

If you use one hand and don't have a good slice backhand, I fear I won't be seeing you in the second round of the club tournament. Don't let a weak backhand hold you back. Be able to jab your opponent to death. Be determined to make it the most reliable shot in your game. The slice backhand will work harder for you than any other shot.

CHAPER 16

THE SERVE

Nothing is more effective in tennis than a powerful serve. Just ask Pete Sampras. He built the most successful career in history around it. If you have a big serve, or are developing one, tennis is an easier game for you because a big serve produces a lot of forced errors. Serving should be an advantage. Ideally, you are hitting a ball with pace, thus giving your opponent little time to prepare. In addition, you know where the ball is going but your opponent doesn't. The problem is that if that good first serve doesn't go in, it isn't going to bother anybody. Unfortunately, this is what I see way too often.

By far, the biggest mistake the Club Player makes is trying to hit the serve *too hard* and *not* getting it in often enough. The result is that your opponent gets to return your much weaker second serve, and what should have been an advantage turns into a disadvantage. The airtight thing to do is to reduce a little bit of power *off* the first serve and get it in *much* more often. If your first serve isn't going in half the time, you're going for too much power. If you're playing really well, it should be going in 70% of the time. So you don't hit it as hard as you can? So what? You still might force a short ball or an error. How often does that happen on your second serve? I doubt very often.

The name of the game at the club level is not hitting a lot of aces, but rather to *not* let your opponent hit your *second* serve. When Mats Wilander won the French Open in 1985, it was a five set match. He did not hit a booming serve, but he got his first serve in 93% of the time! He was not about to let his opponent jump on a second serve on that red clay. That was phenomenal discipline. Copy it! Once again, hail to the Patron Saint.

I'm not saying you shouldn't ever go for a big serve. If you're up 40-love or even 30-love, then maybe you can go for a bigger serve because you've got a little cushion. Conversely, if you're down 40-love, then maybe go for a bigger one, too. But if it's duce, or 40-30, or 30-40, be more careful and get that first serve in. You have a good chance to win that game, so keep the serve as an advantage by getting the first one in.

The single *dumbest* mistake in all of tennis is the double fault. Free points! It can foster snatching defeat from the arms of victory more than anything. What do you think of your team's chances of winning a football game if the other team gets five plays instead of four to get a first down? What if the other baseball team got four strikes instead of three when they batted? Yet, how many Club Players do you know that double fault at least once every service game? Are you one of them? *Stop it*! Can you imagine? All you opponent had to do was stand there and he was rewarded a point.

Tennis Tips and Tall Tales

Here is a scenario I see all too often. You have just played a long, hard point. You had to hit a lot of balls and it took a big dent out of your stamina. Then what happens? You double fault and give the point right back. That's crazy! Unless you have a 100 m.p.h. serve that draws a lot of errors, you *can't* give away free points. They are too hard to win. If you are playing an important match and you are struggling with your serve, don't be stubborn. Tone it down and get it *in*. Do whatever you have to do to get it in.

In the semi-finals of a French Open match against Ivan Lendl, Michael Chang resorted to serving underhanded to get it in! By the way, he won the match *and* the tournament. How much disdain did Bobby Riggs have for the double fault? He once went for six months straight of non-stop tournament play without one double fault. Think about that the next time you double fault twice in one game.

Where should you hit the serve? You should predominately hit the first serve to your opponent's weaker side; and determining which side is weaker is something you have to discover. Most Club Players have a weaker return on the backhand side. If a player is equal from both sides, then you should move the ball around more so that he can't get into a rhythm.

How do you hit a serve properly? Your grip should be the eastern backhand grip. Virtually *all* good players use this grip, and it's almost impossible to radically improve a weak serve without it. When I see a Club Player serve with a western grip, I know what's going to happen, a lot of double faults. Why? Because it makes you hit down on the ball.

Your stance should be sideways to the net. Your left foot, (for right handers), should be turned slightly in. You should be able to rock comfortably from the front foot to the back foot. The backswing should be loose and fluid. Power in serving should come from rhythm, timing and wrist action, *not* excessive strain. Emphasis should be on a healthy wrist snap. The motion is very similar to the throwing motion. Instead of throwing a ball, you are throwing the racquet head. The correct motion should be hitting *up and around* the ball, following through *around* your waist.

Crucial to the success of a repeatable serve is a consistent toss. An inconsistent toss is the scourge of the Club Player's serve and is the biggest reason for serving problems. Hold the ball gently in your fingertips and release it straight up. It's hard enough to hit a perfect toss, much less one that is moving from left to right or front to back. Toss the ball slightly in front of you so that your weight is going forward into the hit. Picture a huge clock face. If you were to extend the racquet straight above your head, that would be twelve o'clock. Toss it, (if you are right handed), to one or two o'clock. The eleven o'clock toss is a fault waiting to happen because it makes you hit off the back foot and swing down. Toss it high enough, so that when you hit it, you are at full extension.

Want to know what separates levels of players more than anything? It's the quality of the *second*

Tennis Tips and Tall Tales

serve. The worst habit out there is the patty-caker, who just taps the ball in. Don't get me wrong; that's always better than a double fault, but it's not a good shot, and it's holding your game way back. That ball goes in with no pace or depth, and gives your opponent all the time in the world to put you on the run or put the ball away on you. You must develop the courage and confidence to take a complete follow-through in order to finish like the first serve with a follow-through around your waist and not facing the net or downward.

The key to the success of a quality second serve is *spinning* the ball. *All good players spin the second serve.* Cut the ball mildly, with a slightly open face, and impart sidespin. This allows you to swing harder and keep it in. If you know how to do this but aren't good at it, by all means practice. If you don't know how to do it, then get someone to show you. It will do wonders for your consistency. Hit the second serve four or five feet over the net. Allow for enough *margin of error.* If your second serve is weak, it would not be a bad idea to spin *both* serves for awhile with the intention of improving your second serve. When your second serve is up to speed, you can then go back to hitting a flatter first serve for more pace.

I hate to face a quality second serve, especially from a left-hander. The spin can be almost as difficult to deal with as a good first serve. The best second serve you will *ever* hit is the one you don't have to hit because the first one went in. When is the last time you saw someone take a bucket of balls and practice his serve? Can't remember when? Me neither.

CHAPTER 17

THE OVERHEAD SMASH

The motion in this shot essentially utilizes the same stroke as the motion in a service stroke. They are the only two shots that put total emphasis on the *wrist snap*. This shot is harder because you have less time to get into position. It takes more timing. The ball you are hitting is falling out of the sky from different angles every time. The correct way to hit this shot is to be sideways to the net like in the serving position. Usually, you need to take very quick little steps to get into position, and allow room to take one final step into the ball to get your weight going forward. The key to making it like a serve is to create the two o'clock point of contact (for right-handers). This allows you to hit up and around the ball with a healthy wrist snap. Follow through around the waist and not down, just like a good serve.

When should you be aggressive with this shot and when should you not? If you are up close to the net and you have time to get ready, then put it away. End the point! You can angle it to either side or go up the middle, depending on where your opponent is. Don't try too much angle, and don't hit the ball too hard if the situation doesn't require it (i.e. your opponent is way out of the court). Don't hit it any harder than necessary to end the point.

Tennis Tips and Tall Tales

By far, the most frequent overhead smash mistake I see being made is facing the net at contact and *not turning*, causing a lot of netted balls. Be sideways when you hit this shot just like in the serving position. The next biggest mistake is letting the ball get too far behind your head before hitting it. This causes a lot of sprayed balls. If the lob is very high and not deep, and you have time, then by all means, let the ball *bounce* before you hit it. This gives you more time to prepare and is, therefore, a much easier shot. The deeper the lob, the less forcefully you should hit it and the more up the middle you should hit it, perhaps with some spin — like a second serve. The deep lob is *no* time to go for a big winning smash. Just get it back deep and with a lot of *margin of error*.

Do you have a bad overhead smash? You are not alone. This is one of the harder shots in tennis, and the vast majority of Club Players are very inconsistent with it. It is also highly under-practiced. Don't continue to let your opponent get away with mediocre lobs. Get this shot up to speed. Nothing in tennis is more fun or feels better than hitting a great overhead to win the point outright. You need to be hitting your fair share of them.

CHAPTER 18

THE RETURN OF SERVE

I absolutely marvel when I see someone like Agassi return a 130 m.p.h. serve with a full swing. It goes back just as hard as it came! Do you know how much timing this requires? It has to be off the charts. It is probably one of the *hardest* things to achieve in all of sports, much less tennis. However, taking a full swing against your opponent's decent *first* serve is probably the biggest mistake I see the Club Player making when it comes to returning serves. I'm not saying you should never do it, but you can't try it every time; it is simply *too* hard to do.

The high percentage skill that is really necessary is to be able to chip or block the return, especially if you have a one-hand backhand. How do you do it? This should be done by stepping into the ball and taking it early. This is a *locked* wrist shot, and is similar to a net shot with a little more back swing. The key is to *borrow the pace* of the ball that was served hard, and *block* it. Let it ricochet off the racquet. To possess the chip return is to greatly reduce the amount of errors you make on your opponent's first serve. If your opponent is not following the serve into the net, then it doesn't really matter how high you chip your return, as long as you get reasonable depth (past the service line). What you have effectively done with a good chip is to take away

Tennis Tips and Tall Tales

the advantage of the serve, and to reduce the point to more of a ground-stroking contest.

Chipping the first serve back deeply is a non-negotiable skill for the good airtight player. If you don't have this shot, please have someone work on it with you. Nothing discourages an opponent more than seeing his good quality first serve consistently get returned. You are making him work much harder for his points now.

If the first serve coming at you is not really hard, then hit a regular groundstroke and be as aggressive as your timing will allow. A weak second serve by your opponent should be *punished*. You need to take advantage of it. If you can put it away now and then by hitting a winner in this situation, then do it. Don't keep trying if too many of them are going out. At the very least, you need to try and take control of the point by putting your opponent on the run. In tennis it is *always* better to be in control of the point than not to be. By far, you would rather be the "runner" than the "runnee." One of the very best chances to take control of the point is by being aggressive off of your opponent's second serve. Get him on the run. Hit it away from him.

Even more aggressively, if you have the necessary skills, you occasionally can hit an approach shot following your return into the net. It puts your opponent into a low percentage passing shot situation. If you are playing for keeps, and a weak second serve comes to your weak backhand, then run around it and hit your stronger forehand.

Most players count way too heavily on their opponents giving them a lot of forced errors off of their good first serve. When you become one of those annoying players who get every return back, you make your opponent enter a whole new difficult world of having to work much harder for his points.

CHAPTER 19

THE NET SHOT

There is no question that the better you get as a player, the more you should get to the net and end more points. This is really a fun shot that can add a lot of offense to your game. Don't worry about having a great volley until your groundstrokes are proficient. You are better off having a really good ground game with a bad volley than being a mediocre at both. But if your "groundies" have matured, it's time to add a quality volley to your game.

The net shot is a locked wrist shot that has more to do with timing than strength. Here, again, you want to take the ball well out in front of the front leg with a well balanced set-up. The advanced volley is executed with just a slightly high to low punched backswing, maybe back three inches. By far the biggest volleying mistake the Club Player makes is taking *too much* backswing. The more backswing, the more chance for error. If you're going to err on the shot, err on the side of *no* backswing at all. There is nothing wrong with becoming a very proficient block volleyer. After all, when is the last time you saw a brick wall miss a shot?

I was playing a social match in Beverly Hills at the home of Leonard Goldberg, who was the president of 20th Century Fox Studios. Leonard and I were playing producer Larry Levinson and actor Sean Connery. Connery had lost the first set and had missed a lot of balls at the net. During the break he asked me for some help. I told him to try just blocking the ball with no backswing. In the second set he did much better at the net. During the crossover, he uttered in that great deep brogue of his, "Great tip, Laddie!"

Another big mistake I see is letting the ball get too far behind you, which makes you have to muscle the shot. When you volley a ball late like this, you almost always lose depth on the shot. A third mistake I see is running through the shot, hitting the volley in between steps. Don't run through the volley. The closer to the net you are, the better you are when volleying; however, it's always better to be *further* from the net with your feet set rather than to be *closer* to the net with your feet *not set*.

When you have to hit a low volley with the ball below the net, it is, most likely, *not* the time to end the point. Try to block that volley deep; and then approach in closer to the net, hopefully, to end the point with a second volley or an overhead. If the situation requires it, be willing to hit two or three volleys in order to win the point.

Once you have committed to going to the net, there is no turning back. It's too late to change your mind. Don't hit the volley any harder than necessary to win the point. I don't know how many times I've seen a Club Player have his opponent way out of the court, and then miss a volley by trying to hit a very aggressive net shot that went out. All he had to do was just block the ball back anywhere in the court! That's like taking a Learjet down to the neighborhood grocery store when a bicycle would have gotten the job done with better results.

It is a great advantage to have the skill of being able to end points at the net. As you improve as a player, the net should probably come more into play. Should you be following your serve into the net? Only if you are ready for it. You should ease into serving and volleying, if you do it at all. If you don't have a decent volley and a reliable overhead, it doesn't make a lot of sense to be eager about rushing up to the net. Your overly aggressive play will only be exposing some weaknesses in your game. Spend time becoming proficient with the volley and overhead, so that when you get up to the net, you're ready to do some damage.

You hate the net? Don't feel bad. You have some good company. So did Chris Evert. Apparently, Andre Agassi and Layton Hewitt do, too. Their groundstrokes are so exceptional that they camp out in the backcourt, preferring to venture in rarely. The last time I looked, they are both U.S. Open champs. It is not mandatory to be a good net player to have success at the club level. But it surely is better to be good at it than not to be. When should you go in? How do you go in? A lot has to do with the approach shot.

CHAPTER 20

THE APPROACH SHOT

One of the best ways to apply pressure on your opponent, and to play offense in a high percentage, conservative fashion, is with the approach shot. Why high percentage? You're *not* trying to end the point with this shot and you don't need to hit it *hard*. You may hit an approach shot winner, but that should be the exception rather than the rule. The objective is to take a short ball, hit it deep, and follow it into the net. It puts your opponent in a low percentage passing shot situation. This is a subtle, quiet offense.

When should you go in? If you get a ball that is well inside the service line, then you should go in *every time*. If, however, the ball is one or two feet past the service line, going in is *optional*, depending on your skill, your speed, the score, the quality of the opponent, etc. If the ball you are hitting is deep in your own court, you should *rarely*, if ever, follow that ball into the net. If you hit the approach shot short and win the point, you're getting away with one. On the other hand, you can hit a really good, deep approach shot, and still get passed and lose the point. By and large, the deeper you hit the approach, the more you can expect to draw forced errors.

One of the most underrated skills you can develop is to take the short ball and convert it to a *deep*

Tennis Tips and Tall Tales 77

approach shot. Now you are turning on the heat. You have just become the "blackjack dealer" rather than the player.

How do you hit? This is the one shot that has the green light to be hit on the run. You need to get down to the ball sideways and not straight on. Because of the momentum of your movement, this is really a *touch* shot. Remember those slice shots? Now is the time to use them, because the approach shot is a locked wrist shot. The approach predominately should be hit with backspin. You should cup the ball on the strings so that you can *catch* the ball and *carry* it deep into the court. It doesn't need to be hard, but it does need to be deep. A short approach is a bad shot, but it sure beats an error.

The saddest thing in *all* of tennis is to see a Club Player grind out a great point by drawing a short ball, only to then give it away by trying to hit too good of an approach shot. Your opponent was in trouble! He was on the verge of being reeled in but was let off the hook, because of not using enough *margin of error* in the approach.

Most approach shots should be hit down the line, but if your opponent's groundstroke is much weaker on one side than the other, you should go to the weak side almost *every time* you go in. It's up to you to pay attention. Don't try to hit great approaches. Hit decent approaches, and be satisfied that the odds are in your favor. Allow for *margin of error*. Over the long haul it should work out for you. The blackjack dealer doesn't win every hand, does he? Once again, if you don't have at least a decent volley and overhead, I wouldn't be too eager to get up there.

Everyone feels pressure when someone hits a deep approach shot at them. It's hard to keep coming up with good passing shots or lobs. It will be hard for your opponent to do it, too. The approach shot is a great shot to have in your bag of tricks. It is a real indication of your maturity as a player. Good players use this shot very effectively. Mediocre players do not.

CHAPTER 21

THE LOB

This is probably one of the *most* effective yet *under used* shots in the game at the club level. Why is a good lob so effective? The world class player can knock off a great overhead from the bleachers, but most Club Players have a weak overhead! Why not exploit that reality? At least test it. One of the keys to success in tennis is making your opponent hit shots he doesn't want to hit. Believe me, most don't want to hit a lot of overhead smashes.

The January 2003 addition of *World Tennis* magazine listed the all time greatest individual strokes. I was not surprised to see that Bobby Riggs was listed as possessing the greatest lob of all time. I can tell you it was a lot more fun having that lob on my side in a doubles match than having to be on the team that had to chase them down all day. I had my fair share of both.

How should you use the lob? It can be used as an offensive weapon at the world-class level, but at the club level it should be used almost exclusively as a *defensive* shot. It can get you out of a jam from impossible situations. Obviously, a good lob is a *deep* lob. The shorter you hit a lob, the more you can expect to have it knocked down your throat.

How do you hit the lob? The shot itself is an abbreviation of a slice shot, and should be hit with mild *backspin*, opening the racquet face more than you would for a normal groundstroke. It should be hit with a *locked* wrist and, here again, you want to *catch* the ball and *carry* it deep into the court. This shot requires touch and feel, and is harder to do consistently well than it looks. It is a real art form, and one that is not used nearly enough. Even though a short lob is a bad shot, I am amazed how many points are won on bad lobs.

The single biggest tactical mistake I see being made is lobbing to the opponent's forehand side. If you have a choice, *always* lob to the backhand side of your opponent. It makes for a much more difficult overhead attempt. Most Club Players try too many low percentage passing shots when their opponents approach to the net. The right thing to do is to mix it up with a combination of passing shots and lobs, so that you can develop confidence in both shots. By far, the lob is the more high percentage shot; so on those days where your timing is bad, you should lob more.

I have great respect for the good lobber and I dread playing against one. Nothing is harder or more exhausting than having to hit three or four overheads to win a point. If you think this is a sissy shot, then I suspect I won't find many trophies in your den.

CHAPTER 22

THE DROP SHOT

This is the shot that you execute by hitting the ball short on purpose; in fact, the closer to the net, the better. This can be a very effective shot, but you should enter into these waters with caution. The drop shot is difficult to execute consistently and is therefore a low percentage shot for most Club Players. It requires *exceptional* touch and feel. The technique on this shot is to use very little backswing and a *collapsed* grip. By that, I mean that you should almost drop the racquet at the point of contact.

The only time to consider using the drop shot is when your opponent is very deep in the court, or pulled way out of the court; the slower your opponent is, the better your chance of success. If you hit a mediocre drop shot, (one that isn't short enough), against a quick opponent, you're going to lose that point far too often. Bobby Riggs had the best counter drop shot I've ever seen. If you tried to drop him with a mediocre attempt, there was Hell to pay. Trust me on that one.

When I see players who are tempted to use the drop shot too much, it indicates to me that they really don't have confidence in their groundstrokes, and aren't willing to grind out a long point often enough. It is a great advantage to be skilled in all the shots, but before even venturing into this one, you need to make sure that your groundstrokes are very sound.

The drop shot should be used sparingly at best. Don't try it at 30-40 or 40-30. At love 40, or 40-love, it can be used as a tool to make your opponent run a difficult wind sprint, and, therefore, deplete his energy supply. Save this shot as an element of surprise or use it, on occasion, to break up the rhythm of the point, so that your opponent can't get comfortable. I respect a good drop shot. I don't see very many of them.

PART THREE

ASK THE PRO

Doug Dean

CHAPTER 23

SHOULD YOU CHANGE A LOSING GAME?

When I was learning and didn't have great strokes, I was never comfortable, even when I was ahead 5-0. When my mechanics got more and more correct, my attitude changed. I realized that, under pressure, good strokes hold up, and you can have confidence in them. I can therefore now be behind 5-0 and feel that I am still in it. Having said that, if your game plan is not working and you sense that you are probably going down with the ship, it doesn't hurt to try something different.

I was in the first round of the Southern Nevada state tournament and my opponent was the No. 1 player at UNLV. He won the first set 6-0. He was ahead 4-0 in the second set. I couldn't get a first serve in to save my life and he was jumping on my second serve. I switched racquets and, all of the sudden, I could get the first serve in. I won the match 6-4 in the third set. I went on to win the tournament, beating a former Austrian Davis Cup player in the finals. Mainly because I won the tournament, I was ranked No. 2 in Nevada that year. If I hadn't switched racquets, I would have lost 6-0, 6-0 in the first round.

Another time, I was playing in the semi-finals of a city league tournament in Arcadia, California. I was losing 4-1 in the third set. I was serving really well but my opponent's return was killing me. Out of exasperation, I served him a very slow first serve. He missed it. I did it again....another miss! I discovered that this guy hated playing with no pace. I went on to win 7-5. If I couldn't analyze how to play my opponent, I was going down. I won the tournament.

When playing a match with an opponent of equal skill, or even better skill, part of your job is to explore. Find out what your opponent doesn't like to do. If he doesn't like to come in, bring him in some. If he doesn't like high balls to the backhand, hit high balls. If he likes to play quickly, then slow down the time in between points. Try to mix up the pace and not let him get comfortable or into a groove. If you have tried to stay back and out-rally an opponent, but he is just too steady, then it might be time to come in more and take more risk with winning shots. What have you got to lose?

It is extremely satisfying to win a match, knowing that you correctly analyzed how to play your opponent. It is the *discovery* that makes all the difference. On the other hand, because you lose, it doesn't mean that your plan was wrong or that you didn't exhaust other ways of trying to win. Sometimes you're going to lose no matter what you try because your opponent is just too good. There is always someone better. Only one person wins Wimbledon.

CHAPTER 24

WHAT ABOUT PRACTICE?

The way you use your practice time has a lot to do with how you improve as a player. Most Club Players spend way too much time hitting their pet shots in practice. Time is better spent working on your *weak* areas. Let's go over some suggestions.

It is really great to have one or two playing partners who enjoy rallying and drilling. I'm a great believer in long rallies. Jump at the chance to have long rallies with anyone who can do it. It's so great for your rhythm and timing. In practice, if the ball comes up the middle during a rally, hit it with the weaker side. In a match, you should do just the opposite. In rallies, you should be working both on more pace and more depth so that you can incorporate these into your game; but don't be a "Fence Beater." No one enjoys hitting with someone who is wild and sprays the ball all the time. I would rather rally with a steady ten-year-old girl any day than with a fence beating Club Player who is trying to impress me with his wild-ass power.

Your groundstrokes will always be the foundation of your game; you can't get too good at them or spend too much time on them. But don't neglect the other shots. Ten balls at the net, or three or four overheads won't get it done. That might be O.K. if you're warming up for a match; but in your practice sessions, try to hit every kind of shot dozens of times, if not hundreds of times. Spend time bringing your weaker strokes up to speed so that you can execute all of them with reasonably good proficiency.

Drilling is excellent practice. One partner can practice net shots and overheads for fifteen minutes or so, while the other can practice groundstrokes and lobs, and visa versa. Groundstroke drills are great. Go forehand crosscourt to forehand crosscourt, backhand to backhand, forehand to backhand, etc. Drilling is great for your timing. To play at a higher level is to have an *accelerated* level of timing. It comes with practice and regular play.

Most Club Players make the mistake of playing too much and not practicing enough. Some players, on the other hand, practice too much and don't play enough. I love a practice nut, but you cannot practice the emotional aspects of playing pressure points without playing an actual match. You cannot simulate pressure. You have to *experience* it. A good thing to do is to drill all the shots for 30 minutes or so, and then play a set or a match. This way you are experiencing all aspects of the game.

CHAPTER 25

WHAT ABOUT PRACTICE MATCHES?

Be smart about how you play your practice matches. If it is the club tournament or an important match, by all means play to win. Be willing to do *anything* you have to do in order to pull off the win. A match that means something is *not* the time to experiment or to be charitable, because you are now putting your skill to the test. Practice matches, on the other hand, should be used to improve your game.

What am I talking about here? If your opponent has a much weaker side, then don't hit every ball to his weak side like you should in a real match. The smart thing to do in a practice match is to hit most balls to the strong side, so that you have to work harder. If your opponent can't return a good serve to the backhand, hit every serve to the forehand, so that you get to hit more balls. The score may be closer. So what? It's just practice, and you can always go back to playing the weak side if winning in practice is important to you. Go for more winners in practice matches. Take more risk. Practice your offense so that you might have more confidence in it when a real match comes.

In a perfect world, you would have a variety of different opponents to practice against: a left-hander, a big server, a net rusher, a Dinker, a lobber, etc. Playing against different styles makes you a much more well rounded player. You will always beat some people, no matter how badly you play; and some people are always going to beat you, no matter how well you play. You need to make the most of both of these situations, even though the outcome has most likely been predetermined.

It is really great to have three or four opponents who are on almost the same level as you. That way, it can go either way. It's more fun to play a match that you have a chance of winning, but only if you play really well.

Handicapping can also make a match a lot more interesting and enjoyable. When I played Jimmy Connors, he gave me both allies. He had to work harder and I could win some points. He had the greatest return of serve in the history of tennis. One time, I came into the net behind my hopelessly mediocre first serve. After he hit a screaming winner while taking a nap, he replied, "Don't ever come to the net behind that piece-of-s--- serve ever again!" I was well chastised. What was I thinking?

Before he moved back to Virginia, I used to go out to Malibu and play actor Robert Duvall. To make the match more interesting, I would not allow myself to hit a real hard serve, nor let myself ever go into the net. My goal was to win 6-0 with those handicaps. It was a huge challenge because he is one of the better celebrity players. One time I had him 5-0, 30-love, and he won the game, preventing the bagel He did a

Tennis Tips and Tall Tales

victory lap around the court like Rocky proclaiming, "Nobody beats me 6-0 on my court, *nobody!*" (It was pretty funny, but maybe you had to be there.) The very next night, I watched him win the Academy Award in front of the whole world for his performance in the motion picture, *Tender Mercies*. Pretty cool. What do you think he was more proud of? Winning the Academy Award or winning one game off of me? Hard to say! Both were incredible achievements.

Bobby Riggs was the absolute master at handicapping matches to make them interesting. I would often see him spot his opponent three or four games, and he would get only one serve instead of two. I've seen him playing with: a frying pan instead of a racquet, boots instead of tennis shoes, and even with one hand tied behind his back. He once played the CEO of Holiday Inn, Kemmons Wilson, in a handicapped match. Bobby placed twenty chairs on his side of the court. If the ball hit a chair, it was in play. Bobby won, and his prize was a gold card. This card allowed him to stay in any Holiday Inn in the world for free. The only other person to get one of these cards was Billy Graham. How's that for some contrast?

CHAPTER 26

WHY DO SOME PLAYERS NEVER IMPROVE?

Did you ever notice that some people get better all the time and some people play the same every year, never ever getting better or worse? Why is that? I think it has a lot to do with whether your stroke mechanics are correct or not. You have heard the old adage that "practice makes perfect." I don't believe that. What makes perfect is *correct* practice. You can get pretty good at hitting a shot with bad technique if you play a lot, but there is one big problem with it. Bad technique has a ceiling. You can get to that ceiling with a lot of practice, but you can never break through that ceiling. The flaws of bad technique, (hitting off the wrong foot, wrong grip, too much tension, etc), will simply not allow you to break through the ceiling. When I see a pretty good player using bad technique, that player moves well, almost always. Great movement covers a lot of sins in tennis, but the flaws in your technique will not allow for maximum improvement.

Good mechanics, on the other hand, have no ceiling; the sky is the limit. Your only limitations are your ability to move and your practice time. If you are just beginning, don't rush into trying to play at an advanced level too soon, because it can get you into

Tennis Tips and Tall Tales

bad habits. Instead, take a little extra time and develop quality mechanics; it will pay off in the long run. A Hamptons client of mine, Marvin Sheeber, didn't start tennis until his sixties. Rather than rush into playing, he took the time to develop good quality, smooth strokes. Now, after three summers, he can compete favorably with good Club Players who have played for twenty years. You can't fool me. When I see a player who has good mechanics and can execute all the shots with smooth consistency, I know one thing: that person has hit thousands of balls correctly for years. He has earned his game by putting in the time. There are no free lunches.

CHAPTER 27

SHOULD YOU CHANGE AN INCORRECT STROKE?

There is no easy answer for this because it is a very hard thing to do. Ideally, yes, you should change an incorrect stroke, but not unless you are willing to pay the price. You've been hitting that backhand off of the back foot with the forehand grip for how many years? And you're pretty good at it, right? To change that would take a total commitment and more work than you think. I can get you to do it correctly in a lesson, or a practice session, but that's just a bandage. Unless you re-route the stroke hundreds, if not thousands, of times, it *won't* show up in a real match. Why not? Because in a pressure match that means something, you will always, and I mean *always,* hit the shot the way it is most comfortable to you, no matter how bad the technique is.

The real trick is for the new improved shot to show up in the *match* and not just the practice session. That is probably not going to happen unless the new stroke has been sufficiently repeated. Repetition develops the muscle memory you need in order to have confidence in the shot, allowing your new technique to show up under pressure. Are you willing to put the time into changing a pretty good, incorrect swing? Only you can make that decision. It takes

Tennis Tips and Tall Tales

longer and is more difficult than you think. A half-ass attempt won't get the job done. There are no quick fixes. You will most likely have to hit the new improved shot hundreds of times, slowly. If you do the work, you are going to play better. The most tangible result probably will be in hitting deeper balls. You will get out of your practice what you put into it. Would you want it any other way?

CHAPTER 28

HOW ABOUT A GOAL?

Nothing energizes your practice like having a goal. If you are starting out a new year, or a new summer season, having a goal gives focus and purpose to your practice. Whatever your level — it doesn't matter. Set a reasonable goal that will both stretch you and result in tangible evidence of your improvement. If you are a beginner, you will want to move up the ladder at the club. Perhaps your goal is to win one round in the club tournament. Maybe it is to just beat Harold Hotshot or Bill Braggart, whom you have never beaten. I have many clients who play all summer in order to try to win the club championship. I have a client who is trying to get ranked in the top ten in the 60 and over, in Florida. I have another client who is trying to get into the top 10 in the East in the 45 and over. I even have one client whose goal is to take a set off of me. When we first started a few seasons ago, I could beat him 6-0, easily. Then it became 6-2, or 6-3. Now it is 6-4 or 7-5. He can mark his progress by the number of games he is getting. Hang in there, Dave King. I admire your persistence and commitment. I believe next season you are going to take me.

When I was just learning in my late teens, I was lucky enough to have a very good woman player play me a set or two every week. She was ranked 20th in the Southern California Women's Open Division. She was kind to play me, because at first I wasn't much practice. I was determined to get a set off of her if it killed me. She was a great challenge and probably beat me 50 sets before I finally broke through. I couldn't have been prouder if I had won Wimbledon. Set a goal for yourself that you can reach if you push hard. Let that become your own private U.S. Open. It will give you a lot of incentive and satisfaction — it will help propel you to the next level.

CHAPTER 29

WHAT ABOUT LESSONS, CAMPS AND CLINICS?

I believe that anything that motivates you to play and sparks interest is a good thing, and worth your time and expense. I am, however, not a big fan of groups or clinics unless they really work you to death. My biggest problem with groups is that, in most cases, they don't allow you to hit enough balls. Hey, let me tell you — you can diagram a stroke, you can have it demonstrated, and you can talk about it to death. While this may be helpful, you are not really going to get it until you *feel* it; and this comes with repetition, *laborious repetition*. This is why I'm more of a believer in one-on-one instruction and, even then, *only* if you are hitting hundreds and thousands of balls. I hate to see tennis pros standing there lecturing, boring their pupils with their great knowledge. Those pupils need to be hitting balls! Hundreds and thousands of balls!

One of the main responsibilities in my lesson with you is to control the *kind* of ball you hit. I am putting you into a controlled environment in which you have enough time to adequately prepare and execute the shot, with reasonably good stroke mechanics. If you are not hitting at least 50 per cent of the shots more or less correctly, then you are not improving sufficiently for the amount of time you are investing in

Tennis Tips and Tall Tales

practice. If I'm hitting the ball too deep or too hard, then improvement just isn't going to happen. Muscle memory needs to *feel* success. Nothing enhances development of hand-eye coordination and muscle memory like slow repetition of correct technique, repeated hundreds and thousands of times. The great golfer, Ben Hogan, called it laborious trial-and-error, (referring to his work on the driving range), and I couldn't agree with him more. I'm sorry — there is no getting around it. As soon as you have a handle on how to hit correctly, then you don't really need lessons; that is, provided that someone continues to hit easy balls to you, so that at least 50 per cent are hit correctly. At first, you cannot hit enough easy balls,

When I was teaching at the MGM Grand Hotel in Las Vegas, Andre Agassi's father, Mike Agassi, was a Maitre d' at one of the showrooms. He would get me into the shows for free if I would hit balls with Andre's older brother, Phil, or his sister, Rita. Mike Agassi was not a tennis pro. He was an Iranian Olympic boxer. He was also a human ball-tosser. I watched Mike toss hundreds of easy balls to five-year-old Andre, Jr. (laborious repetition). Andre got so good, that at age five, he could rally with Jimmy Connors!

Venus and Serena Williams' father was not a tennis pro. He got a shopping cart and filled it with used balls purchased for five cents a piece. Williams became a human ball-tosser for his girls and he created the two best players in the world. Remarkably, he did this in the ghetto.

If you want to put yourself into a crash course of rapid improvement, make sure you are hitting relatively easy balls in a *controlled* environment. Hit thousands of them, gradually increasing the difficulty. Don't get caught standing on a court with fifteen other bored people. That's not going to get the job done. You would probably be better off hitting against a wall or a ball machine.

CHAPTER 30

WHAT ABOUT RACQUETS?

Today's racquets are really a marvel. It seems that every year they get lighter and stronger. In the old days, they weighed about fourteen or fifteen ounces and were made out of wood or aluminum. Now, they weigh about ten ounces and are made out of combinations of ingredients that I can't even pronounce. Jimmy Connors won five U.S. Opens with a 90 mph serve. Today, Roddick and others are hitting it 150 m.p.h! We now have women hitting it at 120 m.p.h. Such is the power of the modern racquet. Does this mean you need to rush out and get the latest $300 racquet to take you to the next level? Not necessarily.

If you are a beginner or a lower intermediate, you will not be able to tell much difference between a K-Mart special and a very high-end racquet, because your strokes aren't developed enough. Don't get a high-powered, expensive racquet until you have the proficiency to use it properly. People ask me to recommend racquets all the time. I tell them there are so many good racquets out there now, that you just about can't go wrong with any of them. Just find one that feels right to you and stick with it. Don't be a racquet freak who changes racquets every month in search of the Holy Grail.

What I can tell you is that whatever the racquet, it needs to feel comfortable in your hand. I like a racquet to feel a little heavy in the head. This is what feels comfortable to me. Most people like the racquet to feel light in the head. It is what ever feels right to you. The point is, don't use a racquet that doesn't feel right just because it's supposed to be so much better than "last year's model."

If you're in the market for a new racquet, I highly recommend that you demo several different kinds before you make the decision. Just because a racquet feels good in a tennis shop doesn't mean it's going to feel right when you hit the court. Don't make an impulse buy. Take your time and choose carefully, because it is important that you really like your racquet. It shouldn't feel too heavy or too light, and the grip shouldn't be too big or too small.

If you have a racquet that you are truly in love with, I recommend that you get two or three of them. By the time you want to get another one just like it, it could be discontinued. I know a guy who searched the Internet for months trying to find a discontinued racquet like his own.

The tension of your strings is really important. If they are too loose, it will cause the ball to sail. If they are too tight, it will require a more perfectly timed ball, and you will get a lot of miss-hits. A racquet with strings that are too tight can also cause tennis elbow. Find the tension that feels right for you. This is a very individual thing. John McEnroe likes a string job on the loose side. Borg loved his strings board-tight.

Tennis Tips and Tall Tales

There are no two stringing machines that are exactly the same. For the vast majority of players, the tension should be mid-range between 55 and 60 pounds of pressure. Remember that strings get looser all the time. If it is the start of a new season, a new string job will probably help your game more than a new racquet and cost far less.

If you are a new player or a beginner, or a very infrequent player, you might want to consider an oversize racquet head over a mid-size one. The extra size makes for a bigger sweet spot and allows for more *margin of error*. Andre Agassi and Venus Williams use an oversize racquet head. If it's not too good for them, you don't have to feel bad about it.

CHAPTER 31

SHOW SOME CLASS

Tennis is a social sport. It is not how you make your living. You play for kicks, exercise, and for the competition. To take it seriously is both good and fun. But it is not life and death. Nothing spoils a match more than someone carrying on and making an ass of himself. So you're having a bad day. So what? Is it causing you to miss a house payment? Don't lose like a baby. Take your whipping like an adult. Don't get the reputation of someone who makes bad calls. Believe me, everybody will hear about it. If you're not sure, give it to your opponent or play two. Do you really want a point you're not totally sure about? Don't question a call unless it is unbelievably obvious. Don't be overly complimentary or make a running commentary about every other point. Just be quiet and play.

Get in the trenches and play hard. Play to win but be determined to have a good time, no matter what the outcome. At least you're out there playing tennis instead of mowing the yard! Don't make excuses. "I can't believe I'm playing this bad." (Yes, you can.) "This is the worst I've every played."...(No, it isn't.) So you lose a match. Big deal. Tomorrow is another day.

OK, so you won. Good for you — but don't be an obnoxious, gloating winner. Who did you really

Tennis Tips and Tall Tales

beat? Federer? Does it really matter in the long run? What is more important, ultimately, is how hard you tried and how you conducted yourself in the heat of battle. Nothing makes me feel worse after a match, whether I won or lost, than knowing I acted like a jerk and lost my self-control.

Don't continually ask a better player to play with you. How many times did you go back to that girl at the party and ask her to dance after she said no once? You can take a shot at a better player now and then, but don't be a nuisance about it. They know you want to play. Let them do the asking. They earned the right.

One of the biggest problems in tennis has always been that we all want to play with players who are better than we are. We want to improve the quality of our matches and get better. The problem is, the better player doesn't often want to play "down" and give a free lesson Think about it. What's in it for him is the potential for a bad loss. It's a little bit of a dilemma. Hopefully, the better player will occasionally ask, but let them take the initiative, and if they ask you to play, snap at it! The trick is to be ready when you get the chance. Forget the outcome; you are already the winner by just getting to play. The steadier you play, the more likely you are going to get to play the better player again. Nobody likes to beat a Fence Beater 6-0, 6-0. A better player is more likely to play with you if you make him hit a lot of balls. If you played well enough for your opponent to say he would like to play you again sometime, then you are the winner, even if you lose the match.

Doug Dean

If you can afford it, taking playing lessons from a teaching pro is a good way to play up. It can get you more prepared to play a better player when you get the chance. I do a lot of playing lessons. I make sure that the pupil hits a lot of balls and plays a lot of long points. I did a Pepsi commercial with Connors one time. Afterward, he asked me if I wanted to hit some balls. Are you kidding me? What fun! Do you think I was going to ask a five-time U.S. Open champion to hit with me? Not in this lifetime.

PART FOUR

THE GREATEST STROKES I'VE EVER FACED

Doug Dean

Tennis Tips and Tall Tales

For an ordinary teaching pro, I've been fortunate to have had the opportunity to hit balls with some of the greatest players of all time. The following is a list of well known personalities whose tennis strokes are among the finest I've had the privilege of facing in a game. Among these are world champion tennis players, sports stars and entertainment celebrities.

The All Time Greats

Serve: Poncho Gonzales and John McEnroe
Forehand: Rod Laver (2 grand slams) and Poncho Segura (3-time NCAA champ)
Backhand: Jimmy Connors
Lob: Bobby Riggs
Net: Roy Emerson (13 majors)
Overhead Smash: Stan Smith (Wimbledon champion), Tony Graham (NCAA champion)
Footwork: Ille Nastase (French Open champion), Vitas Gerilitas (Italian Open champion), and Evonne Goolagong (Wimbledon champ)
Best Sport: Frank Sedgeman (Wimbledon champion)
Most Serious: Poncho Gonzales
Funniest: Bobby Riggs, Ilea Nastase
Craziest: Mac and Connors

Sports Stars

Serve: Rick Barry (NBA) Hall of Fame
Forehand: Mike Warren (3-time NCAA basketball champion at UCLA)
Backhand: Mike Dunlevy (NBA player; Coach, Los Angeles Lakers)
Overhead: Bruce Jenner (decathlon gold medal)

Doug Dean

Net Game: Happy Hairston (Los Angeles Clippers)
Footwork: John Havlicheck (NBA Hall of Fame); Jerry Kelly (golfer)
Best Sport: Joe Torre (Manager, New York Yankees)
Most Serious: Jim Brown (Football Hall of Fame)
Honorable Mention: Frank Gifford (Football Hall of Fame); Oscar Robertson (NBA Hall of Fame)

Celebrity Players

I played a few times with actor Vince Van Patton. He was a child star who left acting to become a world-class player. He is the only entertainment celebrity ever to do so. He got to the round of 16 at the U.S. Open and actually beat John McEnroe twice in tournament play! He would win in this category in every stroke, as would the late Dino Martin, who was close to world-class at one time. In this category, the winners would be second or third choices.

Serve: Kenny Rogers
Forehand: Robert Duvall; Dabney Coleman
Backhand: William King (The Commodores)
Net Game: Bill Cosby
Lob: Merv Griffin
Footwork: Mike Warren (*Hill St. Blues*)
Best Sport: Clint Eastwood
Funniest: Sean Connery
Craziest: James Caan
Honorable Mention: Alan Alda, Sydney Poitier and Johnny Carson

Tennis Tips and Tall Tales

One of my favorite Clint Eastwood films was.....

"THE GOOD – THE BAD – AND THE UGLY"

With Clint Eastwood at the MGM Grand Hotel in Las Vegas

Good: smooth swing
Bad: jerky swing
Ugly: wild swing

Good: deep ball
Bad: short ball
Ugly: ball that hits the fence

Good: early preparation
Bad: late swing

Doug Dean

Ugly: shorts that don't fit

Good: accurate first serve
Bad: weak second serve
Ugly: double fault

Good: correct grips
Bad: forehand grip on the backhand side
Ugly: western grip on the serve

Good: block volley
Bad: swinging volley
Ugly: swing volley hit late

Good: quick, light-footed
Bad: clodhopper slow
Ugly: piano-on-your-back slow

Good: great focus
Bad: no concentration
Ugly: whining over missed shots

Good: always gives server's score first
Bad: can't ever remember the score
Ugly: arguing about the score when you aren't sure

Good: encourages doubles partner
Bad: instructs partner during the match
Ugly: berates partner during the match

Good: a gracious winner
Bad: a gloating winner

Tennis Tips and Tall Tales

Ugly: giving the guy you beat a lesson on the way back to the clubhouse when he doesn't want to hear it

Good: a gracious loser
Bad: loser who makes excuses
Ugly: loser who throws his racquet and makes a scene

Good: two racquets in good shape
Bad: one old racquet with loose strings
Ugly: wood racquet with a broken string

Good: have a court reservation
Bad: having to wait for a court
Ugly: arguing over whom has the court

Good: seventy-five degrees, slightly cloudy
Bad: serving into the sun and you forgot glasses
Ugly: playing in a bad wind

Good: beautifully groomed clay court or slow, cushioned hard court
Bad: ungroomed clay court or fast, hard court
Ugly: fast, dirty, hard court with cracks in it

With Bobby Riggs at the Dunes Hotel in Las Vegas

With Bobby Riggs at a clinic in the Hamptons one year before his passing

Tennis Tips and Tall Tales

With John McEnroe in Nike commercial at the Los Angeles Tennis Club

With Jimmy Connors in Pepsi commercial

With headliner Andy Williams at the Dunes Hotel in Las Vegas

With Merv Griffin at the MGM Grand Hotel in Las Vegas

Tennis Tips and Tall Tales

With Motown magnate Berry Gordy at the Dunes Hotel

Backstage at Caesar's Palace with Berry Gordy, Diana Ross, Bobby Riggs, Gary Collins and Mary Ann Mobley

With Gene Hackman flying his bi-plane in Mexico

At the home of Kenny Rogers with Johnny Carson and Spencer Segura during The Gambler Invitational, Bel Air, California

Tennis Tips and Tall Tales

10,000 feet up on Mount Ararat in Eastern Turkey with expedition mate Robbie Gowdey

PART FIVE

THE ADVENTURES OF A NO-NAME TEACHING PRO

Doug Dean

Tennis Tips and Tall Tales

Tennis has taken me to a lot of different places, and from time to time, I got thrown in with a lot of interesting characters. As I look back, it feels like I have a little of Forrest Gump in me, in the sense that I, too, seem to have had an odd brush with numerous historic tragedies, some involving the bizarre.

~

In the mid 1960's, I played on the high school tennis team at Kimball High School in Dallas, Texas. I was just getting started and wasn't very good, but I had been all-city in basketball. (Not bad for a little white guy, huh?) We played our tennis matches in Kiest Park. One-half mile from the park had lived a crazy radical. He shot and killed a motorcycle cop, and ran for cover in a theater in my neighborhood where he was arrested. He was killed two days later, but not before being accused of an even bigger crime. His name was Lee Harvey Oswald, the alleged assassin of John F. Kennedy. The policeman he shot was Officer J. D. Tippett, whose son was a fellow classmate at my high school.

~

I played college tennis at Pasadena College in California. I had an apartment a couple of blocks off campus with two other guys. One day, I came home from tennis practice and, all of a sudden, there were at least fifteen police cars swarming upon my neighborhood. What was going on? Something terrible had just occurred at the Ambassador Hotel in downtown L.A. Robert Kennedy had just been shot. Who lived a few blocks from me? Sirhan Sirhan, his alleged assassin. Could I be the only person in the world who lived in the neighborhood of both Kennedy assassins?

Where I currently teach at the Bath and Tennis Hotel Resort in the Hamptons, a regular client of mine is a very pleasant lady by the name of Joanne Cohn. She always has a smile on her face and is fun to work with. Since the season is over on Labor Day, our last lesson in 2001 was on September 5th. One week later, on September 11th, Joanne's son was killed in the Twin Towers. I can never hear "911" without feeling deep sorrow for Joanne and her loss.

~

Dr. Alan Roberts of Beverly Hills, California, is a real tennis enthusiast. He is a former 35 and over national champion. He has been gracious enough to allow me occasionally to use his exceptional court to teach private lessons. Dr. Robert's son, Danny, was on the Beverly Hills High School tennis team. Sometimes I had to kick some of Danny's team members off the court so I could teach my lessons. There was one cocky kid who, to me, seemed to personify the obnoxious Beverly Hills brat. I kicked him off a few times. You may have heard of him — Eric Menendez.

~

Tennis Tips and Tall Tales

In Santa Monica, California, where I live half of the year, I try to keep in tennis shape by going up and down a set of two hundred wooden steps that go to the ocean floor. The steps are one block from my apartment and it seems like everyone from my neighborhood works out there. Every now and then I used to see a big guy working the steps. He lived a couple of buildings down from me and drove a white Bronco. His name is Al Cowens, O.J. Simpson's famous protege. The Mezzaluna restaurant, where O.J.'s wife, Nicole Simpson, left her sunglasses, is on San Vicente Boulevard. I live on San Vicente. On a few occasions, I saw O.J. Simpson jogging on my street with Marcus Allen.

~

One morning, I was on my way to the Dunes Hotel in Las Vegas for a 9 am lesson. When I got there, I saw a huge billow of smoke across the street. The MGM Grand Hotel was on fire. It was awful. People were jumping from high floors. Several people lost their lives that day.

~

I flew with Kenny Rogers to Aspen for a pro-celebrity tennis tournament. Kenny and Bjorn Borg played in a special exhibition match on center court against John McEnroe and Marty Raines. Marty was a real estate magnate and tennis nut. He had organized the event. Years later, Vitas Gerilitas was a guest at

Raines' summer mansion in South Hampton, New York. Vitas took a nap in the guest room by the swimming pool. He never woke up. He died of gas poisoning coming from the swimming pool heater in his guesthouse. I was ten miles down the road teaching tennis in West Hampton at the time.

I had played with Vitas at Berry Gordy's home in Beverly Hills. He was perhaps the quickest player I ever saw, and certainly one of the best volleyers. He had won the Italian Open and was a U.S. Open finalist. His death shocked the tennis world. Jimmy Connors was one of the speakers at his funeral.

~

One morning at 4 a.m. in Santa Monica, California, I was awakened by a rumbling noise. It didn't go away. It got louder and louder. My refrigerator fell to the floor and my windows exploded. It was a major earthquake. I knew my ceiling couldn't take a lot more and I got out of the apartment, along with everybody else in my building. Two buildings down from mine a building collapsed and no one was allowed back inside to get anything.

~

Remember that jet that went down after leaving the New York airport the summer of 1999? There was a huge investigation into whether it was shot down or whether it was a technical malfunction that caused it to crash. It exploded just 10 miles south of my beach in

Tennis Tips and Tall Tales

West Hampton. All summer long, I heard sad tales of people finding shoes, wallets, etc....washing up on shore.

~

As I mentioned earlier, Dino Martin was a very good tournament player. He spent two years flying all over the world trying to get a world ranking. I played him a few times. I could beat him but it was always close. One particular week, we had been scheduled to play a singles match at Kenny Roger's home on a Thursday in Beverly Hills. On Tuesday, Dino lost control of a military jet he was flying and flew it into the side of a mountain. He was killed instantly.

~

Enough about sad stories. I hope I haven't depressed you. Let's get a little more upbeat here! On occasion, I would find myself in some unusual match situations in various locations. Here are a few that stand out in my memory:

I was walking through the Caesar's Palace tennis shop in Vegas during the Alan King Tennis Classic one year, when I spotted the great reclusive Wimbledon champion, Lew Hoad, lacing up some sneakers for a legends match. We started chatting and he mentioned that he didn't have anybody to warm him up. I volunteered and he said, "Mate, let's have a go at it." *Cool.* While we were hitting on one of the backcourts, former U.S. and French Open champion, Tony Trabert, asked if he could join us. As if this weren't enough of a kick, up walks the greatest player of all time, Rod Laver, and asks if he can join us. *Sure, Rod, but only because you asked so nicely.* All of the sudden, I'm on the court with three legends of tennis, all at once! I had stumbled onto the field of dreams and I was loving it! We started drawing a big crowd, and I could hear what everyone was thinking – "*Who's that other guy?*" Hey, if you were a college drama coach, would you like to do a few scenes with Robert Deniro, Jack Nicholson and Dustin Hoffman, at the same time? For a no-name teaching pro, the fantasy doesn't get any better than this.

~

I was in my apartment in Las Vegas on a Saturday afternoon in late September. Bobby Riggs was there and we were getting ready to watch Jimmy Connors playing Bjorn Borg in the finals of the U.S. Open. The match was going to start in about one hour. The phone rang. It was Connors! He wanted to speak with Bobby. He had just received the news that Borg had a blister on his thumb that might affect his play. He wanted to know how Bobby thought he should approach the match. Bobby told him, "Jump on him. Try to beat him bad in the first set. Try to break his spirit early."

What Connors didn't know was that Bobby had just bet $1,000 that Borg would win. Borg had experienced a lot of success against Connors in recent months. As much as Bobby liked Connors, there was no reason to believe that Borg's recent domination

Tennis Tips and Tall Tales

wouldn't continue. *Unless.* Unless Borg had a problem — like a bad thumb. We jumped in the car and I drove Bobby back to the Sports Book place. He changed his bet from Borg to Connors. Connors won the match and Bobby won his bet, thanks to one well-timed phone call from the horse's mouth.

Two days later, Connors was in Vegas staying with my former boss, MGM Hotel tennis pro Lorne Kuhle. They came over to my hotel (the Dunes). Bobby challenged Jimmy to a set of doubles for twenty dollars. Jimmy and Lorne Kuhle gave Bobby and me a two-game spot, and Connors only got one serve. (Bobby was in his late 60's at the time.) We beat them 7-5. How many balls do you think Connors got to hit? What, do you think we are crazy? Did that make me the real U.S. Open champ? Kind of? The golf pro at the Dunes was my boss at the time. He heard that Connors was playing on our courts and ran over to watch the set, scratching his head in disbelief. The guy who just won $500,000 for winning the U.S. Open in front of 60 million viewers was yelling and screaming with no shirt on, playing for twenty bucks. I couldn't blame my boss. Hey, I didn't see Jack Nicklaus playing a round of golf with him two days after winning the Masters.

~

One of the fun things about teaching tennis in Vegas is that literally anyone could walk through the gate for a lesson. It ran the full gambit. Everyone, from U.S. Senators and corporate CEO's, to showgirls, gamblers, mob guys, and famous entertainers all came out to hit a few balls. I always liked it when the sports stars came around. It was a real kick to teach the likes of Frank Gifford, John Havlicheck, Oscar Robertson and Joe Torre.

One day, in walked the great running back, Jim Brown. He asked me if I wanted to play a set. I had always heard that Jim Brown liked to beat the pro wherever he went. I don't make a habit of giving my time for free. He had his game face on. (*Hey Jim, YOU WANT A PIECE OF ME?*) I decided it was time to defend my turf. He was very fast and very steady but didn't have good technique, so his shots lacked depth. He couldn't hurt me. I proceeded to drop shot and lob him, and to run him up one side and down the other — over, under, around and through. I kept the ball in play on purpose, and acted like I wasn't trying. I literally ran him into the ground and bloody wasted him. Oh, I beat him 6-0. After the set was over, I asked him if he wanted to play another one. He meekly said "no" and left in haste. (*Hey, Jim, I sure wouldn't want to suit up and try to tackle you in the open field, but I'm not letting you come to MY house and beat me at MY game.*) I can't remember when I enjoyed a set more.

~

Some of the matches didn't turn out that well. Once, when I was teaching at the MGM Grand, famed songwriter Burt Bacharach was headlining with Dionne Warwick. He came out for a doubles match at the Las Vegas Country Club with Bobby Riggs, me and another

Tennis Tips and Tall Tales

teaching pro. During the match, a helicopter started flying low, hovering around the clubhouse and occasionally over the tennis courts. To our amazement, the second time it came over us, Burt Bacharach dove under the bench on the court for protection. He feared there was a sniper in the helicopter out to get him. Yes, this really happened. He freaked out. When the helicopter left, he sheepishly came out from cover, a little embarrassed. He didn't see the humor of it, but the rest of us did.

~

Robert Duvall and I were playing a doubles match with James Caan and another teaching pro on a private court in Beverly Hills. Caan was having a terrible time getting going, and we were killing them. I was looking to encourage Caan when he finally hit a good shot. I said, "That was a really good forehand!" He said to me, "Who are you, Howard Coselle?" Sorry James. I was out of line. No good deed goes unpunished.

~

In the 80's I occasionally got to participate in pro-celebrity events. On one occasion I was playing in an event at the La Costa Resort. I was assigned to a big guesthouse along with Gene Hackman, Merv Griffin, Clint Eastwood and a couple of other teaching pros. It was a Friday night and the tournament was to be over the weekend. At dinner that night, Merv Griffin and Gene Hackman got into a friendly, spirited debate as to who could beat whom. It kept going on and on when, finally, Hackman said, "OK — let's settle this thing." So, at *midnight,* we played on center court under all the lights. Gene and I played Merv and a teaching pro. We didn't finish until 2 a.m. We lost.

The next day I was sitting with Clint Eastwood during a break in between matches. One of the fans was screaming for Clint to give her an autograph. She was in a roped off area up above the courts. As she was leaning down to give Clint her program for him to sign, she accidentally started spilling her Pepsi on him. I couldn't help but laugh as Clint exclaimed in that great "*Dirty Harry*" voice, "Lady, could you try and get it together with the drink and the pen?"

~

I had been teaching for three hours in the bright Las Vegas sun when I was summoned to play a match in the indoor club at the Tropicana. Bill Cosby and I played Kenny Rogers and his movie producer, Kelly Junkerman, who was a former tennis pro and ranked player. I had played with Bill a few times before and it had always gone okay. But coming from the bright sun outside to darkness inside and from a slow court to a fast court, I couldn't hit a ball for the first set. Let me just say this: The great humorist was not humored in the least. To say that Bill was not pleased would be an understatement. *Sorry again, Bill, I really sucked that match.*

~

Tennis Tips and Tall Tales

I grew up I small towns in Kentucky and Indiana. Movie stars were bigger than life figures to me. My favorite film, by far, was *Ben Hur*. I must have seen it fifteen times. Later, during my junior year in college, I had just moved to Southern California and had landed a job as the weekend shop boy at the famed Los Angeles Tennis Club. Because I worked there, I was allowed to occasionally play there during the week. One time, I was there looking for some action, when one of the members approached me with, "Hey young man, they need a fourth on center court — Wanna play?" *Count me in.* I walked out onto the famed court to meet my partner. It was Charlton Heston. Too much.

I still remember one point. I hit a good first serve, came in and hit a good first volley, and then closed in to finish the point with a winning volley at the net. Charlton Heston commented, "Just like it was diagrammed in the textbook." "Thanks, sir," I said, "and you did a good job in that chariot race in Rome." I had been destined to find out that my hero, Ben Hur, had a pretty good forehand.

~

I played in a celebrity tournament in Georgia, and in one of my matches I came up against the all-time home-run king, Henry Aaron. Know what he did in the warm-up? He hit one over the fence. I guess some habits die hard.

Doug Dean

~

After I was graduated from college, I went to Europe to play tournaments. On one occasion, I played in a small event in a little fishing village in Sweden. I lost in the first round to the No. 10 player in Sweden. He gave me a real butt whipping. There was a fifteen-year-old kid in the tournament who caught my eye. I couldn't believe how good he was. He watched me throw Frisbees in front of our hotel. He had never seen one and joined in for a few tosses. The kid won the tournament. The next year he broke through on the international scene. He went on to win the French Open six times and Wimbledon five straight times. His name? Bjorn Borg.

~

I was a teaching pro for a year at a beautiful club in The Netherlands. Inter-club competition is a big deal in Europe and I played on the top-class team at our club. It was like being back on a college team and it was a blast. I had only been there a week and didn't have a car yet, so one night I borrowed a bicycle and peddled a mile to a pub. When I left to go home at 11 p.m., it was raining. It was a heavily wooded area. I became disoriented and completely lost. Everyone in The Netherlands speaks English. But all of the sudden, nobody could. I had peddled into the Twilight Zone. I peddled all night long in the rain. It was 5:30 a.m. when I got back to my flat. Mercifully, a driver had finally steered me in. The sun was coming up. I must have peddled fifty miles to get home one mile. At 7:30

Tennis Tips and Tall Tales

a.m. my team came and picked me up for a road match. My legs were so shot that I tripped and fell during the warm-up for my match, having to default. I was no good to my tennis team that day, but I was more qualified for the Tour-de-France.

~

While teaching in Holland, my favorite pastime was to take my rusted-out, old V.W. bug convertible and go play a tournament somewhere on the weekends. On one occasion, I went to play in a quaint German village. It was a draw of thirty-two (31 Germans and yours truly). I played singles and doubles. I was having a good day and finally lost in the quarterfinals late that evening. It was my *fifth* match of the day. (Three singles and two doubles.) I was still in the semis in doubles on Sunday morning. I will never, ever, ever, *ever* forget how sore I was on Sunday morning. I could hardly walk. I don't know how I got through my match (which I lost). At the cocktail party, they were serving sandwiches. My sandwich tasted a little funny. I checked it out and discovered it was made of raw bacon. When I went to leave, the tournament director came up to me and put two hundred dollars worth of German marks in my pocket. Was that prize money or was it pity? I don't know but I took it. I was sore for a week.

~

Some of my tennis adventures took me off of the court.

    I first met Gene Hackman at a celebrity tournament in Lake Tahoe, Nevada. He was doing a movie in Mexico. He sent a plane for me and two other pros from Vegas to come down for a weekend of tennis. His game left a little to be desired and he jokingly accepted his nickname of "Hackerman." Little did I know that Gene is an avid amateur pilot. He owned a biplane. Know what that is? It looks like one of those WW II fighter planes that requires the use of goggles and a helmet because the air hits you in the face. Gene took me up for a flight. He was piloting the plane right behind me. I couldn't hear a word he said unless he spoke through a microphone that I could hear through earphones I was wearing. He would say, "OK, Doug, we're going to bank to the left," and then we would turn left. After a little while, he said, "Are you ready to do a 360?" "*Huh*?" I said. I looked up and I saw the ground! All of the sudden, I was doing flips in a tiny plane with an actor as my pilot! I'm thinking, "*Hey, Gene, I sure hope you know what you're doing!*" Are you kidding me? It was an amazing, exhilarating, off-the-charts experience. Later at dinner, Gene told me that he had dropped out of high school and joined the Army. At the age of 30, he was selling pots and pans door-to-door in a little town in Illinois. With that background, he went on to become Gene Hackman, Academy Award winner. What a country, huh?

~

Tennis Tips and Tall Tales

A convention and reunion for astronauts was held at the Dunes Hotel where I was the pro, and I met astronaut Jim Erwin. (He walked on the moon!) A year later, I was invited to join a mountain climbing expedition of his, thanks to a mutual friend, Robby Gowdey, who was also on the team. About fifteen of us climbed Mount Ararat in Eastern Turkey. We went there to look for Noah's Ark. Jim Erwin conducted a church service in which he read from Genesis, Chapter 8. It reads, "And the ark of Noah rested on the mountains of Ararat." I looked around and we were 15,000 feet up on the Mount. Too good. I camped out one night on an awesome ice glacier, the same one on which famed French explorer, Ferdinand Navarro, had found a piece of petrified wood years earlier.

Jim Erwin had a little of Indiana Jones in him, and while we were there, he attempted to climb to the summit of the mountain at 17,500 feet to place an American flag. In the attempt, he fell down the side of a glacier, seriously injuring himself. It was getting late and we *couldn't find him*! Turkish soldiers assigned to protect Jim searched all night with torches, to no avail. Everyone was freaked out, to say the least. He was found early the next morning, all banged up. His front teeth had been knocked out and his head was swollen like a pumpkin. He had to be flown by helicopter to a military hospital four hours away in Ezerum, Turkey. The story made all the national wires but ended our expedition. By the way, we didn't find the Ark. Otherwise, I think you would have heard.

~

At the height of Kenny Rogers' stardom there was always a lot of security everywhere. On one occasion, I was staying at Kenny's 40,000-sq.-ft. mansion in Beverly Hills. I was always given a security code to get in and out of the house. Idiot me. I punched in the wrong code number and walked in the front door. The alarm went off and two security guards appeared out of nowhere, with *sub-machine guns* pointed at my head. Wouldn't just one have been enough to take me out?

Another time, I was playing golf at Kenny's farm. It was a weekend and I was the only person staying on the entire 650-acre estate. I did it again. This time it was the fire alarm, and I didn't know how to turn it off. His farm was out in the wilderness 15 miles from Athens, Georgia. Within thirty minutes, 14 fire trucks were pulling up in the driveway. Nobody knew who I was and it looked like I was a prowler or arsonist.

Another time, back in Beverly Hills, I came in at Kenny's house at about 12:30 p.m. I bolted through the back door into the kitchen. All of the sudden, I hear a blood-curdling scream! Country-singing star, Dottie West, was in the kitchen making a pie. I startled her half to death. She had jumped a foot. She didn't know anyone else was staying there and thought I was a burglar. We had a good laugh. I went to her show a couple of times in Vegas after that. A few years later she was killed in a tragic car accident.

~

Tennis Tips and Tall Tales 139

Talk show host Merv Griffin occasionally filmed his show at Caesar's Palace in Vegas. He would always come over for some tennis. I was teaching at the MGM at the time. Merv invited a couple of us to play in a big pro-celebrity tournament in Puerto Vallarta, Mexico. We flew down with him in his plane. I was excited to be playing. We went to a big cocktail party on a Friday night. Later, in the middle of the night, I woke up sick as a dog. I spent the next two days puking, and it was the worst case of the runs I've ever had. I didn't hit one tennis ball, but I hit the john twenty times. I can't ever remember being so miserable before or since. I lost ten pounds. It was not my favorite tournament but it certainly was one of the most memorable.

Seven or eight times, Merv sent his plane for me and MGM tennis pro Lorne Kuhle to fly up to Carmel to play a three-out-of-five set match. Merv and I would play Lorne and Clint Eastwood. It was a very close "mixed" doubles match and I would often go to 7-5 in the fifth set. Merv was known as "Sky King" because he lobbed all the time. Eastwood was known as "Tick Man" because of how often the ball would hit the frame of his racquet instead of his strings. We played that match in four different cities and it always went down to the wire; this was always a real kick. I went right at Eastwood at the net dozens of times, and I must have drilled him at least ten times. He loved it and he was a very good sport.

I was with Eastwood one time at a tournament in Lake Tahoe. We went water skiing early one morning before the matches. I drove the boat for Clint while he skied. He was awesome. When it was my turn, I jumped in and got the shock of my life. Are you kidding me? Trust me — the waters of Antarctica in the dead of winter cannot be colder. Those ice water dousings that football coaches get after a big win would feel like a warm bath by comparison. A group went out skiing again the next day. Guess who took a big pass?

~

On occasion, I would accompany Bobby Riggs at a celebrity tournament. One time I went with him to a tournament in San Francisco. Since I was not playing in this particular event, I was not given a room, so I stayed with Bobby in a room with two beds. He was snoring so loudly that I couldn't believe it. Can you say *foghorn*? I woke him up — I threw pillows — I threw shoes — I yelled. Nothing worked. Finally, I took blankets and slept in the bathtub, but still it was so loud I couldn't sleep. That was a long, miserable night. I never went anywhere with him again without having my own room.

~

I've been at the Bath and Tennis Hotel Resort in West Hampton, New York during the summer months for several years. It's a very long drive from Santa Monica, California. I no longer do it and this is why. I had an old Porsche that I had fixed up. One day, I was cruising along, happy as a lark, without a worry in the world and making good time. All of the sudden I blew the engine. I was five miles outside of Odessa, Texas. Did you ever try to get parts for an old Porsche in Odessa? I had to leave the car there all summer and fly to New York.

The next year I was smarter. I got a reliable Toyota convertible. I took off from Santa Monica figuring I had about a four-day trip. As I was happily driving along without a worry in the world and making good time.......you guessed it; I blew the engine! Where did it happen? Five miles outside of Odessa, Texas! The *same* tow truck picked me up! The *same* mechanic worked on the car. I had to leave *that* car there all summer and fly to New York. I had driven into the Bermuda Triangle. Isn't it a fool who makes the same mistake twice? I now keep a second car on the East Coast.

~

I have never been too keen on betting on a match; it usually causes bad blood and isn't worth it. I make it a point not to go beyond playing for drinks or dinner. Bobby Riggs, however, was a different breed of cat. He had a hard time trying to win unless there was some money riding on it. In fact, he would rarely play anything unless there was some form of a wager. He had received so much notoriety from his match with Billie Jean King, that everywhere he went, he was getting challenged to compete in anything and everything. He had turned into the Pied Piper of action. Bobby was always playing something; whether it was tennis, golf, backgammon, poker, free throws —

you name it, and he would play it, often for pretty high stakes.

Once I was hitting some balls with Bobby at the indoor club at the Tropicana Hotel. Two courts down, a couple of thirty-something high rollers from Mexico City had stopped to watch. They were good tournament players and they approached Bobby, challenging him to a $10,000 three-out-of-five set match. They said that Bobby could use anybody in Las Vegas as his partner. *Bad idea.* Little did they know that the No. 47 player in the world, Jeff Simpson of New Zealand, was visiting the MGM pro, Lorne Kuhle. Bobby recruited Jeff and, after the cash money was deposited in the casino cage, the match was on.

Bobby was steady as a rock and Jeff was too good; they won 6-2, 6-3, 6-2. The amazing thing was this: the Mexicans came back three hours later and wanted to play again in a two-out-of-three set match for another $2,500. Hello? Don't you get it? *Not smart.* This time, Bobby won 6-2, 6-1. That's the most money I've ever seen anyone play for in a live, "whip-out-your-cash" bet. But that was just tennis. Bobby once won $100,000 in a golf match in Florida.

Remember the famous Snake River Canyon jump? Famed motorcycle dare devil, Evil Knevil, was attempting a very dangerous jump over a Grand Canyon-like river in Montana. It was to be televised on pay per view. Well, Evil was even crazier than Bobby; and he bet him $25,000 that he couldn't get to the Snake River from Las Vegas on a little motor scooter in the 24-hour time frame leading up to the big jump.

Tennis Tips and Tall Tales 143

Bobby penciled it out that if he went all night and nothing went wrong, he could barely make it. I watched him take off in front of the Tropicana Hotel. Sure enough, he just made it and collected the big check. His wrist bothered him for two months from having to goose that little scooter all night long.

Another time, a crazy long distance runner named Bill Emerton challenged Bobby to a marathon across Death Valley in the dead of summer. The contest was this: Bill had to complete a 50-mile run before Bobby could finish 25 miles. Sugar Daddy put up the $25,000 prize money for the winner. Again, Bobby had penciled it out and figured he couldn't lose if he could stay at a certain number of miles per hour at a brisk walk or mild jog pace. *Sports Illustrated* covered the race. Bobby wanted some company on the race, so guess who got recruited? We covered 25 miles in 105-degree heat! Bobby won by about thirty minutes and collected another big check. What did I get out of it? Free dinner. If you were crazy enough to bet against Bobby for anything, you deserved to lose.

~

I met Nancy Richey in Dallas through a mutual friend. We had both lived in Ft. Wayne, Indiana for a brief time. I had tremendous admiration for what she had accomplished in her outstanding career. In the 1960's, she was the No. 1 woman in the United States four times. In 1965, she and her brother, Cliff, were both ranked No. 1 in the United States at the same time. This is the only time it has ever happened in tennis history. I was at a U.S. Open in the early 80's watching matches, and I bumped into Nancy again. She was there to try to win the 35 and over national title. She didn't have anyone to warm her up, so I did it for two or three of her matches. Nancy breezed to the finals, but then she had a problem. She had to play against a woman who essentially had a man's body. Dr. Renee Richards had undergone a sex change operation, from man to woman, and was allowed to play in the women's event. That happens every day, right? Nancy lost to the unusual doctor in the finals. But I still think Nancy was the best "woman" in the event.

~

A few of the lessons that I taught don't exactly fall into the category of "normal."

One year, Berry Gordy, the legendary Motown Record founder and czar, drew me as his partner in the David Jantzen Celebrity Tournament at the Riviera Hotel in Las Vegas. We reached the finals. After that, he flew me to his Beverly Hills home to teach him for a week. He videotaped the sessions and at night he would review the tapes on a giant screen. Before the film started, a big title card came up on the screen that said, "A Day of Tennis with Doug Dean." I got a big kick out of that. It looked like I was starring in a major motion picture. One day, Diana Ross came to watch. Another day, Smoky Robinson stopped by. His assistants all referred to him as "The Chairman."

Tennis Tips and Tall Tales

Berry took me on a tour of his studios at Motown Records. Want to see some people snap into action? They snapped for Berry like nothing I've ever seen. I was told that he often worked late into the night and had trouble sleeping. One morning, we were having breakfast, getting ready for a morning tennis session. Right in the middle of a sentence, he leaned his head down on the kitchen table and fell asleep. His assistant waved me off and whispered for me to "let the Chairman sleep." Needless to say, on that morning there was no "Day of Tennis with Doug Dean."

Berry takes his tennis very seriously and he plays very well. He was a big fan of Bobby Riggs. He really wanted to play with Bobby Riggs and I regret not ever being able to put them together in a match. The "Chairman" is a very cool dude.

~

It was the end of a very long day of teaching in Las Vegas under a 95°, cloudless sun. My patience was thin and fatigue had begun to set in. A guy with a Latin appearance came out for my last lesson of the day. He was quiet and very shy, and his English was not the best. He was very stiff with his stroking and I tried to get him to relax. I even went over to his side of the net and grabbed his arm and slapped it, trying to get him to loosen his grip. I think I terrified him (Maybe rightfully so.) Toward the end of the hour, I finally got him to hit the ball a little better. As he was leaving, he said he wanted to play again the next day. I asked him what business he was in. He meekly said that he was in the clothing business. I wished him good luck, thinking that he would need it.

The next day was Sunday, and there was a three-page story about the excellence of a fashion show from one of the famed designers visiting in town. Sure enough, it was the shy man whom I had slapped around. The next day, he asked if I would be the head pro at the resort hotel he was building in the Dominican Republic. He said to call him in two weeks in New York. When I called, I had to go through four assistants to get to him. (Is it that hard to get to President Bush?) When I was finally put through to him on the line, he apologized and told me that his partner had given the job to someone else. Who got the job? Six-time Wimbledon doubles champion and U.S. Open champion, Tony Roche. *I hate to lose a job to someone less qualified than I am.* Oh, well, easy come, easy go. Congratulations to Tony. Just so you know, I could play the best match of my life against Tony Roche, and he could get off his deathbed with a broken ankle and a sprained wrist, and beat me 6-0, 6-0 without even trying. If he hadn't gotten injured early in his career, he would have been one of the best players of all time. But that doesn't mean he's a good coach, right? All he did was coach Ivan Lendl to the finals of the U.S. Open *eight* years in a row. He currently coaches the best player in the world, Roger Federer. Oh, yeah, who was the designer? Some "obscure" guy named Oscar de la Renta.

~

Tennis Tips and Tall Tales 147

Another designer came out for lessons every year for three years. He had to be in his 70's, and every year he had a different, young, beautiful girl with him. Hey! Am I in the wrong business? He spoke with an Italian accent. He was always talking about his friend, Jackie Kennedy. I didn't like his tennis line of clothes, but they sold all over the world. He played pretty well. One year he won the pro-celebrity that preceded the U.S. Open. His name was Oleg Cassini.

~

A family act was entertaining at the MGM Grand Hotel while I was teaching there. A couple of the brothers came out for lessons. They wore high top basketball shoes and basketball shorts. These guys were good athletes. We hit it off right away because we were all born in the same town, Gary, Indiana. The youngest brother was twelve and very shy. He watched from outside the fence and had a big "fro." His name was Michael Jackson.

~

While teaching at the Bath and Tennis Hotel in West Hampton, a very cute lady took a series of five lessons while on her summer vacation at the beach. She was a crime reporter for a local news station in New York. It was fun to work with her and we even went out for drinks a couple of times. There was only one problem. After she left, she "forgot" to pay me. I called her a couple of times. She apologized and said

Doug Dean 148

the "check was in the mail." The third time I called, the cel number didn't work anymore. Neither was there any response to the letter I wrote to her. *"Hey, Channel "X" News, I'd like for you to cover a robbery.. Could you send your crime reporter out here? One other thing — could you make sure she brings her checkbook?"*

~

One day a spoiled little rich kid from Beverly Hills came out for a lesson, watched by his father. He was about ten years old. After missing the first ten balls, he threw the racquet down and ran into the corner of the court where the two fences came together. He just stood there hiding his face and pitching a fit. The father nervously waved his hands at me and whispered to me, "It's okay — I will pay you." I could see that he was afraid of his precocious child. I got paid for a half-hour lesson that lasted all of thirty seconds. I could get used to that.

Speaking of short lessons......

At the MGM, a guy came out for a lesson and his drinking buddy came along to watch. After about five minutes into the lesson, the boozed-up pal started disagreeing with what I was teaching. After a few more remarks I got a little impatient and said, "If you think you can do better, than *you* take over." He said, "OK, I will." He proceeded to take my racquet and teach his

Tennis Tips and Tall Tales

friend for the remainder. I just sat there, relaxed, and didn't say a word. Twenty-five minutes later I said, "OK, time's up. Lesson is over." He proceeded to pay me for watching him teach my lesson for half an hour. Go figure.

~

I had another very short lesson. One time, while at the MGM Grand, the wife of one of the most famous sports stars in the world came out for a lesson. (No, he has not been mentioned in this book.) I could tell you who the star was, but I would have to kill you, or beat you 6-0, whichever is worse. To prevent myself from turning into the *National Enquirer*, he will be my Deep Throat. The wife was a well known New York supermodel. She and I hit balls for five minutes and she said, "Do you mind if we just sit down and chat for awhile?" Hey, it's OK with me — the meter is ticking. She proceeded to confide in me that she was becoming unhappy and disillusioned with her marriage. I was a total stranger and she spilled her guts to me for half an hour. She invited me to go to lunch because her husband was playing golf. I knew it was not a good idea, so I said goodbye at the gate. Two months later, I was sorry to read that she had filed for divorce. Was I surprised?

~

While at the Dunes Hotel, I was teaching a guy from Miami for a few days. He was pretty good. Ironically, my next pupil was with a first timer who was also from Miami. He, too, was not a bad player. I casually mentioned to the second pupil that I should put him together with the guy who had just taken a lesson, so that they could play together in Miami. Innocent enough, right? Well, this guy responded like he was going to have a nervous breakdown. He was convinced that the first guy was sent by his wife to spy on him during their divorce proceedings. He told me to "name my price" to fill him in on what the other guy was asking about him. When I told him I didn't know what he was talking about, he didn't believe me! It took me a full thirty minutes to convince him of my innocence. It wore me out and I felt like charging for the therapy session. How's that for paranoid?

~

I feel it is a part of my job to encourage every pupil and to be very patient. This especially holds true with the ones who are struggling and having a hard time. One day while giving a lesson to a lady at the MGM Grand, I was tested to the max. I was on one side of the net with my teaching basket and she was a very short distance from me on the other side. I gently tossed the balls to her with my own hand. I did this for ten minutes but she did not hit a ball once. I tried everything I could think of, only to get the same result, a complete whiff on every ball. Wow! I went to her side of the net court and stood right beside her. I dropped the ball right next to her. Whiff, whiff, whiff. I tried everything, with no result. She went the entire thirty minutes without experiencing the sensation of her racquet touching the ball. The one thing I was not

Tennis Tips and Tall Tales

willing to do was hold the ball in my hand and let her swing at it, although she probably would have missed it. That was the only time in approximately 10,000 hours of lessons that I ever saw this happen. I used to say that anyone can learn. *Not anymore.*

The following is a true story without any exaggeration or embellishment. I was teaching a middle-aged lady at the Dunes Hotel. I like to watch a pupil hit for awhile before I say anything, just to get a feel for his strengths and weaknesses. With this particular lady, I hit 25 balls to her forehand. Her form was reasonably good and she only missed one or two balls. I hit 25 balls to her backhand. Her form was bad and she missed every ball. Tactfully, I said, "Well, it looks like we might want to concentrate on the backhand to see if we can bring it up to speed." She said, "But that's wrong. My backhand is my best stroke." *Excuse me?* Let me get this straight, I was saying to myself, you hire me for my time and experience. You assume that I am a pretty good player and know at least something about teaching the mechanics of the strokes. Theoretically, I'm on your team and here to help.......right? Know what I did with her? I *agreed*. I said, "Oh, okay.....well then, let's work on that weak forehand." I proceeded to hit balls to her good forehand for thirty minutes. When someone is crazy, I'm not going to fight it.

There are two basic requirements that all pupils should have to adhere to: (1) you should show proof that you were born on planet Earth and not from Denial Land, or (2) disclose whether you've ever been in an insane asylum and, if so, that you have recovered enough to function in the real world. I'm not sure which of these requirements that this lady didn't pass, but I promise you — it was one of them.

~

I hesitate to mention this one. What the heck. I'll give it a shot. I was teaching a guy at the MGM how to hit a serve. I demonstrated it and broke it down, and now it was his turn. When he hit the serve, I heard a funny noise. I chose to ignore it. Three serves later, I heard it again. Are you kidding me? The noise was emanating from his backside, and there is a term for it that rhymes with "dart." Now, what am I supposed to do? I've got a guy who's serving and letting them rip! He didn't say anything, so I didn't either, but I had to bite my tongue and look away. I was grateful for the session to end because I knew I was going to lose it at any second. I should not make fun of a poor guy who obviously had a bladder problem, but when he walked out of that gate, I had to laugh hard for five minutes just to get it out of my system.

~

Another interesting character came out for some lessons while I was teaching at the MGM Grand. He told me that he owned recording studios in Miami. He was flamboyant, to say the least. He loved tennis and wanted to fly me down to Miami during a slow week in January. *Did you ever do anything when your instincts told you not to do it?* So, January came and I flew to Miami. This guy had a beautiful home and boat

Tennis Tips and Tall Tales

on the water. We played a lot of tennis during the day, and at night we did the town.

On a Wednesday night, he said that he had a "business meeting." Something didn't seem right about all of this. He was being too secretive. I was getting a bad feeling. As it turned out, my client did own a recording studio, but what he did from there was broadcast his "sermons." He turned out to be an Elmer Gantry type of preacher. He was a white guy with an all black congregation who sold "prayer cloths" on the radio. You could buy them and get your prayers answered. Apparently, business was good. Count me out. *Count me out.* I got out of Dodge as fast as I could.

~

I have a friend, Joe Pytka, who is the world's premiere TV commercial director. He is a sports nut and does most of the great Nike spots. On Super Bowl Sunday, half of the commercials are Joe's. When there is tennis involved, he sometimes calls me to help out. He did a commercial with John McEnroe and my job was to be John's off-camera opponent. We filmed on the famed center court of the Los Angeles Tennis Club. Joe had never seen me play and was worried about my ability to keep up with "Big Mac." They taped us playing points. We played for about an hour. I could tell Joe was relieved that it had gone well. Afterward, a reporter interviewed McEnroe about the commercial and his article appeared in the *L.A Times* the next day. When asked about me, Mac said, "I don't know who that guy was, but it was like hitting against a human backboard." Pretty cool, huh? Nice to get a little acknowledgment from one of the greats. I also like it that he didn't know who I was, because that's who teaching pros are: no-name guys laboring in obscurity. I often watch Joe Pytka shoot commercials with his crew, and I always got more respect from the crew after that session with Mac.

~

Remember those Nike "Bo Knows" commercials with Bo Jackson? Joe called me in to work with Bo on the tennis part of that commercial. I was at the net hitting easy balls to Bo. Joe started making fun of him, telling him that he hit like a girl. Well, Bo got annoyed with that and started hitting the ball as hard as he could. The more Joe egged him on, the harder he hit it. Do you have any idea how strong Bo Jackson is? The balls were spraying off the camera, the walls, the trucks, the catering tables, and everywhere. He was hitting them like they were shot out of a cannon. When Bo would swing, everybody on the crew would dive for cover like army guys trying to avoid an incoming grenade (including yours truly). Thank God for that net. I dove under it every time, but I half-way expected the ball to come through the net and take me out.

Tennis Tips and Tall Tales 155

**With Kenny Rogers in the Broadway Christmas production,
"The Toy Shoppe" (I was Doug the Deliveryman)**

Playing tennis on the road with *The Gambler*

Tennis Tips and Tall Tales

On the Road with The Gambler

I met Kenny Rogers in Las Vegas in the early 80's. I was a fan of his successful pop singing group, The First Edition, and I would watch them in the Hilton lounge. Kenny came out to the MGM one day to play. Thereafter, he would call when he was working in Vegas and we would play everyday. Then his career exploded. Kenny had become a tennis nut and he wanted someone to train with him full time. The Dunes Hotel gave me a hiatus. For the next two years, I hit the road with *The Gambler*.

I could write a whole book about my adventures on the road with Kenny. It was a heady experience. He was on a roll with seven straight hit songs. When Kenny hit the height of his stardom, he was doing 250 shows a year. My job was to line up an indoor club at the next city on the tour, and arrange a doubles match with Kenny, myself and the local pro or club champs at that club. We would often play three or four different teams, starting at 10:00 a.m. in the morning and go until 2:00 a.m. After lunch, Kenny would take a nap and then go do the show. Every night backstage, the teams we played would come hang out and see the show as Kenny's guests.

Ever wonder what it would be like to get into a limo and have a police escort to a private jet? We did it *every night*. There would be a pizza waiting on the jet, and in five minutes we were out of there and onto the next town. Sometimes, on the spur of the moment,

Kenny would have the limo driver pull into a McDonald's on the way to the airport. Can you picture six motorcycle cops (with lights flashing) waiting for Kenny to knock down a Quarter Pounder with cheese before we could continue onto the plane? By the way, we're not talking a little pansy Learjet here — we're talking a DC-9. In case you can't picture that, it was bigger than Air Force One. It took three pilots and, most of the time, there were only two passengers. I lived on that plane for two years. It had sleeping cabins, kitchens, all the latest games, and every gadget known to man. James Bond had nothing on us. I was living *large*.

Every tennis club we went to drew a big crowd when we showed up. Sometimes there would be several hundred fans waiting outside the club, and one or two local film crews to catch a glimpse of *The Gambler*. The fastest I ever saw Kenny run was not on the tennis court, but rather when he was running back to the limo outside the tennis clubs as the fans were chasing us. One time, we flew into Rockford, Illinois. Kenny was to be the first superstar ever to appear at the new arena there. There were 10,000 people at the executive terminal waiting just to see him land. Now we're talking "Beatles" action. I could have walked off that plane, naked, and nobody would have noticed. Needless to say, it seems like I've seen every indoor club in the United States, and I know I've been backstage in every major arena.

There were several occasions when I would have friends at the show that lived in the particular city where the show was playing. After the show, say in

Tennis Tips and Tall Tales

Chicago, Kenny and I would fly back to his farm. I would then call my friends to see how they liked the show — and they wouldn't even be home yet. I was already in bed in Georgia and they were caught in show traffic.

Here is a sampling of some fun things I got to do:

Kenny arranged for 20th Century Fox to put me on the crew of his feature film, *Six Pack*, with Diane Lane and Michael Hall. I was a "production assistant." The minute Kenny finished his last lines of the day, we would *helicopter* to the nearest indoor tennis club and play. The crew hated me.

The film crew of *60 Minutes of Australia* traveled with us on Kenny's plane to shoot an episode on Kenny. They taped us playing and talking tennis aboard the plane and backstage. Two years later, Kenny and I played an Australian former Wimbledon champion, Frank Sedgeman. He told me that he had seen me on "60 Minutes!" You gotta love it when the Wimbledon champs notice you.

I flew with Kenny to the world premiere of *Six Pack* at the World's Fair in Knoxville. Sherry Lansing, president of 20th Century Fox, met us at the airport and we went with her to the theater. When we got out of that limo, there were at least two hundred photographers flashing. It was like walking through a fireworks display.

Doug Dean

We got to play a lot of great players. We sat down and figured it out one day that we had played twenty Wimbledon champions.

At Kenny's home in Beverly Hills, two or three times a year, we would have round robin tournaments. We called the event, "The Gambler's Invitational." It would usually be a teaching pro teamed up with a celebrity in a "mixed doubles" format. Some of the celebs included: Johnny Carson, Robert Duvall, Sidney Poitier, Alan Alda, Berry Gordy, Bruce Jenner and Robert Loggia. It was always a blast, and the winning pro got a nice check.

One day, we were playing with Evonne Goolagong in Miami. Kenny had a show that night in North Carolina, but was having such a good time that he didn't want to leave. Hey, it was five o'clock in Miami and Kenny had an eight o'clock show — and we're playing tennis. We're cutting it a little thin, here! As bad luck would have it, the limo driver got disoriented and couldn't find the executive terminal where the plane was. Now, it's 6:30 when we take off. Kenny is supposed to be in the arena two hours before the show to be safe. People were walking in the arena in North Carolina already.

The flight was ninety minutes. When we landed, the limo and police escort were waiting. Kenny changed in the limo and walked straight from the limo to the stage without stopping. Keep in mind, we had played three hours of tennis in the hot, tropical sun, sweating like pigs. Without showering, he put on his

Tennis Tips and Tall Tales

suit and walked on. I made it a point not to get near the first three rows that night.

One time, we were on the road somewhere in Florida. Kenny was doing an interview, so I rode over to the arena with a couple of ladies accompanying Kenny on the trip who were interior decorators. On this particular tour, there was a young, green comedian for the opening act. He asked if he could ride over with us. Sure thing. The problem was that we got stuck in the show traffic and were proceeding at a snail's pace. Eventually, it became evident that we were not going to make it on time. The comedian was not going to be able to do his act. So the girls asked him to do his show for us in the limo. He was great. I cracked up. It wasn't so funny when we got to the arena, though. Tour promoter C.K. Spurlock read the riot act to the comedian. The comedian recovered nicely and went on to do pretty well for himself. His name was Jerry Seinfeld.

Starting again in the mid 90's, I had been traveling with Kenny as his tennis coach during the months of November and December on his Christmas show tour. It was like the old days, except for one thing. He wrote a holiday musical called "The Toy Shoppe" in which there was a small part that required someone to play "the deliveryman." Since I was already on the tour for tennis duty, Kenny asked me to play the part! Now I'm not just watching the show every night; *I'm in it*

The next year, Hallmark brought the show to New York. We did 65 shows at the Beacon Theater on

Broadway. The three-week rehearsal in New York for the show was a pretty intimidating process. All of the sudden, I'm out there with trained Broadway singers and dancers. I will never forget how freaked out I was on opening night. Picture this scene: there were telegrams, flowers everywhere, reviewers, the whole nine yards. I'm backstage and I'm thinking that I'm getting ready to do what ten thousand more qualified starving waiters in New York had been trying to get to do their whole lives. I had to go out and sing, dance and act to a packed house at the Beacon Theater, with friends in the audience. It was scary and bizarre, and an altogether out-of-body experience for me. At the end of the show, I helped roll a sign on stage. What would inevitably happen shortly thereafter was that 5,000 people would give us a standing ovation. I can tell you this — in 25 years of teaching tennis, nobody ever clapped after a lesson was over. I could get used to this. Nathan Lane, eat your heart out. Don't worry; I didn't give up my day job. But it was amazing what the skill of being able to keep a few tennis balls in play had allowed me to experience.

Over the years, some of the opening acts for Kenny included: Garth Brooks, Amy Grant, The Gatlins, B.J. Thomas, The Righteous Brothers, Dolly Parton, Brooks and Dunn, Trisha Yearwood, Crystal Gayle, Glen Campbell, The Oak Ridge Boys and a whole host of others. Often, one of the other entertainers would fly back with us to the farm for some golf, tennis or fishing.

Kenny built an awesome eighteen hole golf course on his farm that he designed. He planted 5,000

Tennis Tips and Tall Tales

trees. It was nothing for us to play 54 holes in one day. One time, I played 125 holes in one day with the University of Georgia basketball coach, Hugh Durham.

Kenny was a great ambassador for tennis. He put up all the money for the College Tennis Hall of Fame at the University of Georgia in Athens. Recently, he sold his farm and moved to Atlanta.

Kenny has a very funny, self-deprecating sense of humor. I've probably had more hard laughs with him than anybody I know. He worked hard on his tennis and he became good. On his best day, he could play doubles at a very high level. He is also a good actor, writer, and a world-class photographer, with three published books. Oh yeah, he has also managed to sell *one hundred million albums* and he has had a hit record in six different decades! That's not what you call a flash in the pan.

Is your boss doing well financially? During the height of his career, my boss played tennis all day and worked for one hour a night, with one hundred days off during the year, and managed to knock down 35 million dollars annually. Not bad work, if you can get it.

The most impressive thing about Kenny to me is how he conducts himself. Every night backstage, he met dozens of people, yet when he would get out of the limo at the end of the night, he would thank the driver by name. I hadn't had a thing to do all night, but couldn't remember the guy's name. I have seen hundreds and hundreds of drivers, waiters, security guards, front desk clerks, etc....leave with a big smile on their faces because *The Gambler* had made them feel good about themselves. Kenny Rogers is a class act. To be affiliated with him was, and still is, a privilege.

~

Tennis has given me a lot of adventures, and I hope it gives you some great ones as well. Hopefully, our best adventures are yet to come. I hope I have motivated you to think smarter about your tennis game. So, if you're ever in the Hamptons, or if you ever hear that Kenny's Christmas show is coming to your town, track me down and let's hit some balls. Remember — cut down on those unforced errors, and allow for a healthy *margin of error*. Play within yourself; play airtight! Now, get out there and sneak up on some people who have been beating you. They wont' know what hit them. They will think they are having a bad day, not realizing you are making them work harder. When you get one of those wins because you've played smart and competed so well, I hope it makes you smile. I also hope you remember 'ole Bobby and the no-name teaching pro. Email me with your airtight win story at dougdean@magicvalleypub.com. I will smile with you.

About the Author

Doug Dean was a small college All-American and formerly ranked No. 2 in Southern Nevada. He has played tournaments in ten different countries and has taught over 15,000 hours of private lessons in Beverly Hills, Las Vegas, Miami, New York and Europe. In Las Vegas, Doug taught at the MGM Grand Hotel and was the head pro at the Dunes Hotel under Tennis Director, Bobby Riggs. He was graduated from Point Loma College in San Diego, California with a Bachelor of Arts Degree in psychology. Doug currently is the head pro at the Westhampton Bath & Tennis Hotel Resort in West Hampton Beach, New York.

www.ingramcontent.com/pod-product-compliance
Lightning Source LLC
Chambersburg PA
CBHW031249290426
44109CB00012B/500